The U.S. Naval Institute on
MARINE CORPS AVIATION

U.S. NAVAL INSTITUTE
Chronicles

For nearly a century and a half since a group
of concerned naval officers gathered to provide
a forum for the exchange of constructive ideas,
the U.S. Naval Institute has been a unique
source of information relevant to the nation's
sea services. Through the open forum provided
by *Proceedings* and *Naval History* magazines,
Naval Institute Press (the book-publishing arm
of the institute), a robust Oral History program,
and more recent immersion in various cyber
activities (including the *Naval Institute Blog*
and *Naval Institute News*), USNI has built a
vast assemblage of intellectual content that has
long supported the Navy, Marine Corps, and
Coast Guard as well as the nation as a whole.

Recognizing the potential value of this
exceptional collection, USNI has embarked
on a number of new platforms to reintroduce
readers to significant portions of this virtual
treasure trove. The U.S. Naval Institute
Chronicles series focuses on the relevance of
history by resurrecting appropriate selections
that are built around various themes, such as
battles, personalities, and service components.
Available in both paper and eBook versions,
these carefully selected volumes help readers
navigate through this intellectual labyrinth by
providing some of the best contributions that
have provided unique perspectives and helped
shape naval thinking over the many decades
since the institute's founding in 1873.

THE U.S. NAVAL INSTITUTE ON
MARINE CORPS AVIATION

THOMAS J. CUTLER
SERIES EDITOR

Naval Institute Press
Annapolis, Maryland

Naval Institute Press
291 Wood Road
Annapolis, MD 21402

Library of Congress Cataloging-in-Publication Data
Names: United States Naval Institute, author. | Cutler, Thomas J., 1947–,
    editor of compilation.
Title: The U.S. Naval Institute on Marine Corps Aviation.
Description: Annapolis, Maryland : Naval Institute Press, [2016] | Series: U.S.
    Naval Institute chronicles | Includes bibliographical references and index.
Identifiers: LCCN 2015047124 | ISBN 9781682470404 (alk. paper) |
    ISBN 9781682470411 (mobi)
Subjects: LCSH: United States. Marine Corps—Aviation—History.
Classification: LCC VG93 .U5595 2016 | DDC 359.9/6—dc23
    LC record available at http://lccn.loc.gov/2015047124

♾ Print editions meet the requirements of ANSI/NISO z39.48–1992
(Permanence of Paper).
Printed in the United States of America.

24 23 22 21 20 19 18 17 16   9 8 7 6 5 4 3 2 1
First printing

CONTENTS

EDITOR'S NOTE

BECAUSE THIS BOOK is an anthology, containing documents from different time periods, the selections included here are subject to varying styles and conventions. Other variables are introduced by the evolving nature of the Naval Institute's publication practices. For those reasons, certain editorial decisions were required in order to avoid introducing confusion or inconsistencies and to expedite the process of assembling these sometimes disparate pieces.

Gender

Most jarring of the differences that readers will encounter are likely those associated with gender. A number of the included selections were written when the armed forces were primarily a male domain and so adhere to purely masculine references. I have chosen to leave the original language intact in these documents for the sake of authenticity and to avoid the complications that can arise when trying to make anachronistic adjustments. So readers are asked to "translate" (converting the ubiquitous "he" to "he or she" and "his" to "her or his" as required) and, while doing so, to celebrate the progress that we have made in these matters in more recent times.

Author "Biographies"

Another problem arises when considering biographical information of the various authors whose works make up this special collection. Some of the selections included in this anthology were originally accompanied by biographical information about their authors. Others were not. Those "biographies" that do exist have been included. They pertain to the time the article was written and may vary in terms of length and depth, some amounting to a single sentence pertaining to the author's current duty station, others consisting of several paragraphs that cover the author's career.

Ranks

I have retained the ranks of the authors *at the time of their publication*. As noted above, some of the authors wrote early in their careers, and the sagacity of their earlier contributions says much about the individuals, about the significance of the Naval Institute's forum, and about the importance of writing to the naval services—something that is sometimes underappreciated.

Other Anomalies

Readers may detect some inconsistencies in editorial style, reflecting staff changes at the Naval Institute, evolving practices in publishing itself, and various other factors not always identifiable. Some of the selections will include citational support, others will not. Authors sometimes coined their own words and occasionally violated traditional style conventions. *Bottom line:* with the exception of the removal of some extraneous materials (such as section numbers from book excerpts) and the conversion to a consistent font and overall design, these articles and excerpts appear as they originally did when first published.

ACKNOWLEDGMENTS

THIS PROJECT would not be possible without the dedication and remarkable industry of Denis Clift, the Naval Institute's vice president for planning and operations and president emeritus of the National Intelligence University. This former naval officer, who served in the administrations of eleven successive U.S. presidents and was once editor in chief of *Proceedings* magazine, bridged the gap between paper and electronics by single-handedly reviewing the massive body of the Naval Institute's intellectual content to find many of the treasures included in this anthology.

A great deal is also owed to Mary Ripley, Janis Jorgensen, Rebecca Smith, Judy Heise, Debbie Smith, Elaine Davy, and Heather Lancaster who devoted many hours and much talent to the digitization project that is at the heart of these anthologies.

Introduction

IN THEIR COMPREHENSIVE BOOK *The U.S. Marine Corps: An Illustrated History* (Naval Institute Press, 2001) Merrill Bartlett and Jack Sweetman wrote:

> The first instance of a coordinated air-ground attack, later to become a Marine Corps specialty, occurred in August [1919], when a Curtis Jenny and a DH-4 cooperated with an infantry company to surprise a big *caco* camp on a mountain near Mirebalais [Haiti]. The planes' bombs drove the startled *cacos* off the mountaintop into ambushes set by the ground forces, who killed or wounded more than two hundred of them. Marine aviators also began to develop dive-bombing techniques that would enable them to place their ordnance in the confined target areas of jungle clearings.

While the U.S. Marine Corps is well known for its accomplishments in various forms of warfare, most especially amphibious, Marine aviation does not normally enjoy the same limelight as those other forms. Yet, whether flying propeller-driven biplanes or hovering jets, "Leatherneck" aviators have been supporting Marine ground operations since the early days when military aviation made its debut.

The selections from *Proceedings* magazine included in this anthology range from the days of Smedley Butler to modern-day operations in the Middle East. Two of the selections deal with using air power to fight guerillas, and the comparison of Marine air operations in Northern Europe and in Southeast Asia highlights some of the versatility of Marine Air in various theaters.

The detailed discussion of Marine Corps aviation in Vietnam is an example of one of the lengthy articles that appeared in the pages of the *Proceedings* in the days when the May issue (also known as the Naval Review issue) often included very long articles. In contrast, the very short piece on Joe Foss (appearing as a Lest We Forget feature) succinctly recounts the exploits of a Marine who was awarded the Medal of Honor as an aviator—not the first, nor the last.

Two of the articles provide different viewpoints—one an infantryman and the other an Air Force officer—relating to Marine Aviation. The latter discusses what happens when different services—with their different doctrines—come together for the same mission.

In the final piece, Colonel Linn addresses the need for an expeditionary air force in the future and Marine Air's potential role in it.

This eclectic collection serves as both a tribute to Marine Aviation's importance to a wide variety of conflicts and operations and as a stimulant to meaningful thought regarding the future of this lesser-known but vital component of the U.S. Marine Corps.

1 "Smedley Butler's Air Corps: The First Marine Aviators in China"

Gabrielle M. Neufeld and James S. Santelli

U.S. Naval Institute *Proceedings*
(April 1977): 48–59

LESS THAN TWO YEARS after the court-martial of Billy Mitchell, when both the Army and Navy tried to downgrade the use of air power, a Marine general decided to make an aviation unit an integral part of his brigade. He determined that it would function as a significant element in the expeditionary force he commanded. In the summer of 1927, a small group of Marine aviators commenced air patrols over unfamiliar and often hostile territory in North China. Their deployment is attributed to the persistence of Brigadier General Smedley Darlington Butler.

A tide of anti-foreign feeling was sweeping through China in the 1920s. The xenophobia, born from a resurgence of Chinese nationalism, was the cause of anxiety and apprehension in the foreign community. In the years following the Boxer Rebellion, China witnessed a deterioration in the power of the central government. Regional and provincial warlords ruled vast areas of the country as their private fiefdoms. In 1926, however, Chiang Kai-shek, a leader of the Nationalist Party, placed himself at the head of a strong army and embarked on a campaign to reunify China and free it from foreign influence. Moving from their stronghold in the southern province of Canton, Nationalist forces marched north, overwhelming all who dared oppose them.

By fall, Chiang's army had reached the Yangtze Valley in central China and was poised to strike at the cities of Hankow, Nanking, and Shanghai. All three contained numerous foreign-owned businesses. This was especially true in Shanghai which also had the largest non-Chinese settlement in the country. Alarmed at the swift conquests by the Nationalists, foreign residents feared for the safety of their sizable economic holdings and for their lives as well. Urgent appeals for protection were sent to various European nations, Japan, and the United States. Recalling the dark days of 1900 when foreigners were viciously assaulted and their property destroyed, the major powers responded by sending troops and ships.

American concern resulted in the decision to increase the meager U.S. garrison already there. Besides the Asiatic Fleet which regularly patrolled Chinese waters, the United States had a force of nearly 500 Marines at Peking, the old capital, and the Army's 15th Infantry Regiment at the nearby city of Tientsin. These small contingents had been established after the Boxer Rebellion to protect the diplomatic community and to insure a safe access to the sea should there arise a need to withdraw Americans from Peking.

The first troops to deploy were elements of the 4th Marine Regiment which sailed from San Diego in late January 1927. This was the vanguard of an expeditionary force that would number 5,000 Marines within a few months. These men eventually formed the 3d Marine Brigade commanded by Brigadier General Butler, holder of two Medals of Honor and perhaps the Marine Corps' most colorful officer.[1] Butler was no stranger to China. At the age of 19, he had won a brevet captaincy for gallantry in battle at the city of Tientsin during the Boxer Rebellion.

Included in the reinforced brigade were three infantry regiments, part of an artillery regiment, an engineer company, a tank detachment, and an aviation contingent. This was the first time a Marine expeditionary force was accompanied by aviation units. Elements of the Marine Corps' Aircraft Squadrons, West Coast Expeditionary Force were alerted for a deployment to China in late March 1927. A few days earlier, on the

24th, rampaging Nationalist soldiers seized the inland port of Nanking, attacked foreigners, and looted foreign-owned property. American and British warships were forced to open fire on Nationalist troops to prevent further death and destruction. The fall of Nanking and the continued northward advance of the Nationalists caused consternation in the American diplomatic community. Career diplomat John V. A. MacMurray, U.S. minister to China, urged the deployment of a sizable American military force, including a "substantial detachment" of air units. MacMurray felt that aircraft could be well employed, if the occasion arose, because the "... Chinese are ignorant of the effectiveness of this weapon and are apt to disparage it."[2] His telegram emphasized to both the State and Navy Departments the need to include an aviation section in the expeditionary force that was being mounted out.

Orders came quickly for the departure of Marine air units. On 7 April, Headquarters Detachment, Aircraft Squadrons, West Coast Expeditionary Force, commanded by Major Francis T. Evans, and Fighting Plane Squadron 3, under First Lieutenant William J. Wallace, sailed from San Diego on board the Navy transport *Henderson* (AP-1). Also sailing were two Marine infantry battalions and support units. Four days later, the auxiliary ship *Gold Star* (AG-12) departed from Guam with Captain Walter E. McCaughtry and 102 men from Scouting Squadron 1.

Bloody fighting had erupted earlier that month in the Chinese sections of the city. Although the fighting had stopped by the 25th, British, American, Japanese, and Italian troops, along with those from other nations, still manned barricades and remained on guard along the perimeter of the non-Chinese portion of Shanghai. By 3 May, both Marine contingents were in Shanghai with eight partially dismantled Boeing FB-1 fighters. Although the ground troops were off-loaded, no firm decision had been reached on the employment of the two aviation forces. The ultimate determination rested with Admiral Clarence S. Williams, Commander in Chief of the Asiatic Fleet and all American armed forces in China. There was some doubt whether the squadrons would ever fly.

General Butler arrived in late March. After meeting with Admiral Williams on board the cruiser *Pittsburgh* (CA-4), the Asiatic Fleet flagship, in Shanghai, he came away with the belief that the admiral was not willing to use the Marine fliers. In a letter to Major General Commandant John A. Lejeune, Butler asserted that Admiral Williams "... doesn't want to land them, and if he does land them, he doesn't want them to fly, and I want them to do both." The British had offered the use of their landing field, the only one available in Shanghai. But the airstrip could not be used because it would have been too congested with additional planes. Butler also found out to his dismay that the British were restricted by treaty to flying over only those areas of the city controlled by foreigners. The pragmatic general recognized that Williams did not want to duplicate the British effort, and that there might be diplomatic repercussions from overflights of Chinese territory. Butler then subtly persuaded Admiral Williams to send the aviation group to the Philippines to be held in readiness for a possible move to some other trouble spot in China. Knowing Williams' reluctance to use his Marine airmen, the general was thus able to prevent the permanent withdrawal of the air units by agreeing to accept a temporary hiatus with the option of reentry in the future.[3]

Additional personnel and planes from San Diego joined the aviators at the Olongapo Naval Base on 9 May. The strength of the aviation section was now nearly 170 officers and men. Within a month, the squadrons received the remainder of their authorized aircraft. Besides the eight FB-1s, the Marines now had six Boeing 02B-1 observation aircraft and five of the newly acquired Loening OL-6 amphibians. These planes, however, remained in their crates and were not assembled, much to the exasperation of the impatient pilots.[4]

Originally, there had been some confusion in the shipment of the planes and spare parts. Most of the equipment was not shipped with the main contingent of personnel. Artillery materiel destined for the brigade took precedence. A good portion of the aviation equipment, therefore, was left standing on the docks in San Diego to be sent at a later date. This failure in logistics and the subsequent problems in finding a landing field in Shanghai raised, possibly for the first time, the question of whether an aircraft carrier should be assigned to the Marine Corps. Spokesmen for the Corps were quick to point out that the 3d Brigade's aviation force was "of no use" to General Butler upon its arrival in China. Had there been a carrier available, they contended that the planes ". . . would have been ready at a moment's notice to go to any point required . . ." and operate indefinitely, regardless of whether shore facilities were accessible.[5]

The redeployment to Olongapo witnessed the activation of Observation Squadron 5 under Captain James F. Moriarty. It was the first Marine air unit to be formed outside the United States. This completed the structure of Aircraft Squadrons, 3d Brigade which was now composed of a headquarters, one fighting squadron, one observation squadron, and a scouting squadron detachment.[6]

Although his aviators were in the Philippines, Butler refused to abandon efforts to get Marine planes flying in China. The determined general, in fact, wanted more Marines in China, including a reinforced regiment that was being held in Olongapo. He felt it was his ". . . job to put as many Marines as possible into the show in China . . . and will leave no stone unturned to accomplish that end." Admiral Williams, on the other hand, was still reluctant to bring in more troops unless there was a further threat to American lives and property. Moreover, the question of flying over Chinese territory without permission remained unanswered. It appeared that the squadrons would be employed only under grave circumstances.[7]

Minister MacMurray anticipated trouble in North China as early as 29 March 1927 and feared that a Nationalist takeover of the region would be followed by a repetition of the violence that had occurred in the south. Admiral Williams eventually agreed that there was a threat to American interests. He sent General Butler north to survey the area. Butler, of course, was delighted with the prospect of being given a second opportunity to get his Marines into China. His mission to the north and the possibility of his men being deployed there made him feel that the "Old Man" (Admiral Williams) was ". . . going to be a great Marine booster." MacMurray's concern over North China was confirmed by Butler. Both Peking, the capital, and the inland river port of Tientsin were considered in danger of falling. If that happened, Americans in the region would be isolated and left to the mercy of the unpredictable Nationalists.

Contingency plans were drawn up for the establishment of a strong point at Tientsin near the coast so that U.S. citizens could find protection there. Butler remembered the torturous march to Peking to save the diplomatic community during the Boxer Rebellion. He therefore wanted a strong force deployed in the area to keep open an escape route from Peking to the sea, a distance of approximately 90–100 miles. All agreed that the 800-man 15th Infantry Regiment and the Marine Legation Guard in Peking were too small to do the job. General Butler suggested that his reserves in the Philippines be used, and Admiral Williams concurred. The regiment at Olongapo, which was later designated as the 12th, and "every bit" of aviation were ordered to Taku Bar on the Gulf of Chihli some 25 miles downriver from Tientsin. The 6th Marine Regiment and Headquarters of the 3d Brigade which were at Shanghai were also ordered north. Both forces were then to converge on Tientsin.[8]

Between 27 June and 3 July 1927, the aviation contingent was unloaded from the transport *Chaumont* (AP-5) at Taku Bar. Accompanying the airmen were 24 aircraft, including fighters, amphibians, and observation planes. To control the vital Hai River which flows through Tientsin, General Butler selected Hsin Ho, located five miles from the river's mouth, as the site for his aviation base. There the air units and a small security force soon assembled. Butler had wisely chosen Hsin Ho for several reasons. It gave him a base near the sea. With other units located at Tientsin, he could control river and rail traffic from that city to the coast. Moreover, the presence of the aviation force was less conspicuous at Hsin Ho, yet it was only a 15-minute flight to Tientsin.

General Butler, ever mindful of the possibility of arousing Chinese indignation, determined to avoid flaunting his air force. He hoped gradually to win Chinese acceptance by demonstrating that his force was not going to be used offensively but only in the defense of Americans attacked by invading armies. Admiral Williams had cautioned Butler to be discreet in his use of aviation. Both men knew that British overflights of Shanghai had caused a Chinese boycott of British goods, resulting in severe financial losses for English firms. Admiral Williams wanted no similar incident affecting American merchants. The astute Butler pointed out that the agreements following the Boxer Rebellion gave various foreign powers the right to maintain free communication along the railroad between Peking and the sea. A zone two miles wide on either side of the track was allowed for the stationing of troops. It was General Butler's contention that the concords would not be violated by planes flying in this zone. He assured Williams that his pilots would not fly outside the zone and that he would not initiate flights until MacMurray approved ". . . and had broken the news gently to the Chinese Foreign Office." Williams and MacMurray willingly accepted his viewpoint.[9]

A field near the Standard Oil compound in Hsin Ho was designated as the base of operations for the squadrons. The camp was named in honor of Minister MacMurray, which of course did little to hurt the cause of the aviators. MacMurray, in fact, recognized the need for the squadrons insofar as they ". . . would be of inestimable value in maintenance of communication." Most observers felt that there was an ominous likelihood of open hostilities in North China. The battle-hardened Butler readily agreed. He expected that the first American combat planes to be stationed in China were "going to be run to death," if the events predicted took place. Should there be a need to forcibly maintain open access from Peking to the sea, Butler envisioned using his aircraft in a supportive role for Marine infantry and in the defense of the diplomatic community. If the foreign legations were besieged as in 1900, the mobility of the Marine squadrons theoretically would present the Americans with the means of breaking the siege in a short time. A number of aircraft were equipped to carry 163-pound bombs. Most could carry ten 25-pound fragmentation bombs. The planes were also armed with machine guns. Butler foresaw opposition from Chinese aircraft, but he had no fear that his pilots could handle them. In reality, no Chinese army had a viable air arm.[10]

Upon arriving at Hsin Ho, the Marines worked tirelessly to get Camp MacMurray into shape. An airstrip was laid out near the railroad station. With the help of Chinese coolies, part of the field was leveled and formed into a rough runway. The aircraft were uncrated and quickly assembled. Not knowing if there would be an outbreak of trouble, Brigade headquarters ordered its air squadrons to be operationally ready as soon as possible. General Butler in the meantime strived to expand the role of his aviators. Both the Navy and the State Departments had consented to permit the Marines to fly over 120 square miles of land between the northern boundaries of Tientsin and the sea. The general confidently felt he could be able "gradually and quietly" to expand this zone once all concerned became accustomed to flights over the area. He recalled with satisfaction the shift in views of Williams and MacMurray. Originally, they had been dubious at best about Marines flying in China. But now Marine airmen were ashore and about ready to take to the air. It would be only a matter of time according to Butler before they would fly beyond the zone to Peking.

The first flights began in early July 1927. Anxious to learn the status of his air force, Butler decided to make a firsthand inspection of Camp MacMurray. It was nearly his last. Major Evans, commanding Aircraft Squadrons, 3d Brigade, dispatched Captain Arthur H. Page, Jr. to Tientsin to pick up the general. Page landed his 02B-1, a newer version of the World War I–era DH-4B, on a field near the brigade's headquarters. His passenger immediately boarded, and the plane took off. Before landing at Hsin Ho, Butler had Page circle the camp for an aerial inspection. The pilot then came in for a landing, but Page, who was still not familiar with the field, overshot the runway. The 02B-1 finally came to a halt after nosing into a makeshift Chinese laundry that had been set up near the end of the field. Evans and his assembled Marines, fearing a tragedy, raced to the site, only to find that both men had emerged unscathed. After crawling out of the plane, the perturbed general reportedly turned to the embarrassed pilot and gruffly said: "A little close wasn't it? You'll kill yourself someday, Page! Do it when I'm not with you!" Butler's prophetic words came true, for Page died in an air accident three years later.[11]

Shortly after the establishment of Camp MacMurray, Butler began preparations to send his planes to Peking, if necessary. A landing site on the grounds of the city's Temple of Heaven had been selected. Its 737 acres were protected by a strong wall. Unused for years, the once park-like grounds were overgrown by brush and trees. The enclosure, therefore, had to be cleared. In meetings with Chinese officials, Butler marveled at the beauty of the temple area, and remarked that it might be more beautiful if the grounds could be restored. The flattered authorities agreed with the general. The area was soon cleared and put into "first-class shape." According to Butler, the Chinese had thus "unknowingly provided a splendid field" for the aviators should an emergency arise.

As Marine planes began to appear regularly over Hsin Ho, protests from the government in Peking and from local warlords were sent to the 3d Brigade and the American Legation. Butler, undaunted by his accident, continued to see value in the air units. He persisted in efforts to win Chinese acceptance. The warlords had insisted that troops and planes be withdrawn. Butler shrewdly pointed out that the planes could be used for their escape should they be defeated by the Nationalists. After they were taken up in Marine planes to witness bombing practice, those who had been unconvinced were persuaded not to attack American forces. In his dealings with the Foreign Ministry he used a low-key approach. He arranged for important Chinese officials to be given rides in the planes, and protests usually subsided thereafter.

One amusing incident occurred when the Chinese Minister of Foreign Affairs made, through his secretary, an official complaint about the flights. It was done for show only; however, the American consul in Tientsin and the American Legation took it seriously—much to the horror of the Chinese Foreign Ministry. A Chinese emissary was hurriedly sent to General Butler to explain. Knowing the Chinese need to save face, Butler agreed with the official that all future protests would be sent directly to him with the understanding that nothing would be done about them. The Chinese had in fact privately reported to Butler that they had no objection to the planes at all and felt safer with them in the area.[12]

With the tacit approval of the Chinese Foreign Ministry, Butler made plans to openly fly three of his aircraft to Tientsin. He persuaded Minister MacMurray to go along as a passenger in one of the planes while he and Major Alexander A. Vandegrift, a member of his staff and later the 18th Commandant of the Marine Corps, were passengers in the other two aircraft. MacMurray, by now an ardent admirer of the general, decided to make the flight to demonstrate his support for Butler. On the morning of 15 July 1927, three Marine fighter biplanes from Hsin Ho landed at Tientsin and were unexpectedly greeted by 25,000 excited Chinese, most of whom had never been near an airplane. Although the flight had been announced previously, such a large crowd had not been expected.

A few weeks later, command of Aircraft Squadrons, 3d Brigade passed from Major Evans to Lieutenant Colonel Thomas C. Turner. This change delighted Butler who at times had been critical of Evans for being "temperamental." The general felt Evans, the first man to spin and loop a seaplane, was a good flier but not the best commander. In the general's eyes, Evans was a malcontent who had committed the unpardonable sin of going over Butler's head to complain to authorities in Washington. Evans had been dissatisfied with the squadrons' role. Butler was so annoyed by Evans' actions that he was tempted to turn the Marine planes over to Navy fliers. Instead, he suggested that Evans be sent home.

Butler, with a flair for the dramatic, used his veteran fliers to demonstrate their versatility in air shows to impress the Chinese and the foreign community in Tientsin. On 10 November 1927, the Marine Corps' birthday, the 3d Brigade arranged for a special review. Fourteen planes were flown from Camp MacMurray to Tientsin for this purpose. For the foreign residents, at least, it was one of the highlights of the year. One incident that occurred during an air show has long been remembered by those who witnessed it. During an exhibition of stunt flying, Captain James T. "Nuts" Moore made a low pass over the crowd and then went into a breathtaking climbing roll, lost the wings from his aircraft, bailed out, and parachuted into a moat in front of the stands. Most spectators, unaware that it had not been planned, thought it was the best show they had ever seen.[13]

Requests for additional men and equipment for the squadrons were sent to Washington that fall. Most were turned down because of two factors: active Marine air operations against dissident forces in Nicaragua were now taking precedence, and the expected Nationalist attack on the cities failed to materialize. Although the danger of an invasion of North China had eased, Butler refused to be lulled into a state of complacency. The "Fighting Quaker," as he was often known, stressed the continued need for his men to remain alert. As winter approached, however, some thought was given to the curtailment of air activities. The area's harsh climate, especially the icy, cold winds blowing down from Manchuria, made flying hazardous at best. Besides, Marine pilots and crews had little experience in conducting winter operations and had none in flying in zero weather. But Lieutenant Colonel Turner decided against ending flights of his aircraft. This met with the hearty approval of the 3d Brigade commander who appreciated this type of dedication. After an inspection trip to Hsin Ho in December, he called Turner "a first class commander" and praised the "splendid condition" of the planes and equipment. Butler also applauded the men for not having "let down one inch" and was particularly impressed that an entire squadron could still "take the air in 15 minutes, at any time." He gave the mechanics special credit for maintaining the planes in good working order.

In meeting the rigors of the winter, the mechanics devised innovative methods to keep the planes flying. To avoid difficulty in starting water-cooled engines on cold mornings, the men drained all fluids from the planes. The fuel, oil, and water were put in separate drums over fires which burned throughout the night. In the morning, the planes were filled with the warm liquids, thus significantly reducing the time needed to start the aircraft.[14] As the pilots and crews made every effort to keep their planes in the air that winter, the new Commander in Chief of the Asiatic Fleet, Admiral Mark L. Bristol, hoped to bring about their withdrawal. The admiral felt such a move would be seen by the Chinese as a friendly gesture. As might be expected, Butler was against the idea and requested that Major General Lejeune ". . . do something to save our aviation and even increase them in strength, if possible."

Bristol's views were also strongly opposed by both Minister MacMurray and the American charge d'affaires in China, Ferdinand Mayer. The latter warned the State Department that fighting would resume in the spring. Both men, moreover, favored retaining the air units until after the next round of fighting was concluded. Although Bristol considered a withdrawal, even a partial one, as a possible step in improving Chinese-American relations, the other three countered by pointing out that the inevitable resumption of warfare would create new problems for Americans. The air units, as had been argued the year before, could be the deciding factor in a potential crisis. The arguments presented by MacMurray, Mayer, and Butler outweighed those of Bristol. With pressure coming from not only Headquarters, Marine Corps but also from the State Department, the Navy refused to act on Bristol's suggestion, and the Marine aviation contingent remained in China. One change did occur. The number of units was reduced on 31 January 1928 when Scouting Squadron 1's Expeditionary Detachment was deactivated. Personnel were transferred to Observation Squadron 10.[15]

All during the winter, the planes continued to fly routine missions as much as possible. Passenger and mail service was provided between

Tientsin and the coast. When the field adjacent to brigade headquarters was closed because of inclement weather, the pilots used the local racetrack in Tientsin as a landing strip. Weather permitting, pilots of the amphibian OL-6s would ferry mail and supplies back and forth between Camp MacMurray and ships of the Asiatic Fleet at sea in the Gulf of Chihli. Also, the squadrons trained with the other elements of the 3d Brigade to maintain a high degree of readiness. They worked with the artillery units to provide them with a rudimentary form of airborne fire control.

In addition, they moved to establish a workable liaison with the infantry. Marine infantry regiments were fortunate to have a portable radio station mounted on the back of a truck. The vehicle could accompany the troops in an operation. In maneuvers designed to test the feasibility of air-ground coordination, cumbersome sending and receiving sets were placed experimentally in some aircraft. Morse code communications in field exercises between troops on the ground and planes in air were reportedly excellent up to a distance of 15 miles. The innovative connecting link between aircraft and ground troops offered untold advantages to the infantry, should they be ordered to march into hostile territory. Thus, the aviators would not only be the eyes of the advancing infantry but also theoretically would be able to furnish effective air support at the time needed.[16]

In April 1928, Chiang Kai-shek and the Nationalists renewed their drive on North China. Those foreign military contingents in the area, including the 3d Marine Brigade, attempted by various means to keep informed of the Nationalist advance. American planes were already taking aerial photographs of possible approaches to Tientsin. As Chiang's armies drew near, the importance of Butler's squadrons as a reconnaissance force came to the fore. The foreigners knew that Tientsin was a target but did not know when the Nationalists would strike or in what strength. Lacking a sufficient intelligence system and having no air capabilities, the other foreign military commanders in Tientsin envied Butler and his air force. The Japanese, in fact, did bring a few antiquated observation planes into the area, but they proved to be ineffectual in providing information on Chinese troop movements. They were, however, a cause of concern for the Marines when they flew into the zone between Tientsin and the sea. When they entered, Marine fighters immediately took off to meet them and to insure that the Japanese had friendly intentions. Although not sure at first, the brigade determined that there existed little threat from the small Japanese air detachment.

Marine squadrons were initially ordered to conduct reconnaissance over the main roads and railway from Tientsin north toward Peking and south toward the sea for a distance of 20 miles in each direction. Pilots were directed to report on the movements and disposition of all Chinese troops and were instructed to prevent Chinese aircraft from flying over the foreign concessions in Tientsin. Actually, no Chinese planes were in the area. They were given an additional directive to watch for attempts by the Nationalists to block the entrance of the Hai Ho and to attack any force that would try such a move.

In June 1928, the Nationalists began their final drive on the north. On the 4th, they entered Peking and moved to take the city of Tientsin. A day earlier, Lieutenant Colonel Turner had received orders from General Butler to begin immediate daily air reconnaissance patrols and to expand the area covered by the patrols. All planes that were operational were put into the effort, including newly arrived aircraft from the United States, one F8C-1 and eight F8C-3s. These two-crew, fighter biplanes had just been acquired by the Marine Corps in 1928. Turner mustered a total of 31 aircraft: 19 fighters, six amphibians, and six observation planes. Pilots on patrol were cautioned to avoid antagonizing the combatants and were ordered to maintain a minimum altitude of 1,000 feet.[17]

For over two weeks, Marine patrols covered daily a greatly expanded area of 8,000 square miles and reported to brigade headquarters on the location of military columns, the identification of troops, and the locations of military installations. In this brief period, Marine planes were in the air every day from dawn to dusk and logged a total of nearly 1,000 flying hours. A serious difficulty in the observation of the contending armies soon developed. Reports concerning the identification of specific locations were confused and inconsistent. As General Butler later pointed out, the June crisis demonstrated that ". . . all pilots were not good observers." Lieutenant Colonel Turner solved the problem by designating Captain Francis J. Kelley, Jr. and Second Lieutenant Francis B. Loomis, Jr. as specific observers to accompany the pilots. Neither officer was a pilot at the time, although Loomis was a student aviator. Each was sent out on missions twice a day to reconnoiter the front lines. The two men were overworked, but both filed reports that were more accurate than when pilots acted as their own observers. Troop movements, identification of types of troops, the location of troop transports, and the location of staging areas were relayed to brigade headquarters in Tientsin.

In one unusual mission, the pilots were ordered to drop propaganda material over villages and towns in the region. Butler had other plans to have his planes drop leaflets on advancing Nationalist units. These leaflets stated the 3d Brigade's willingness to pay a relatively sizable sum of money for the weapons of any soldier who deserted. Hot meals would also be provided. The program, however, was never implemented.

In flying over Chinese troops of the local warlord, Marine planes were struck seven times by hostile fire, but none was downed, and the fire was not returned. Pilots acted with restraint since they were under instruction not to fire unless there was an immediate and obvious threat to American lives. Marine officers were dispatched to Chinese commanders to explain the presence of the aircraft. The officers returned to Tientsin with the assurance that there would be no further firing on American planes after a description of all Marine aircraft was given to the Chinese. They had mistakenly fired on the planes, believing the aircraft belonged to the detested Japanese. Once the identity of the aircraft had been established, no further incidents occurred. By this time, however, the crisis had terminated. The Nationalists had seized Peking. On

17 June, troops allied with the warlords Chang Tso-lin and Wu P'ei-fu abandoned Tientsin to the Nationalists and withdrew northward. Apprehension that the city would be attacked by the Nationalists proved to be unfounded. Air reconnaissance patrols were discontinued the following day. With the Nationalists in firm control, an uneasy peace settled over the Tientsin area.

Butler's squadrons had kept track of approximately 250,000 Chinese troops in June. While gaining valuable experience in reconnaissance work, the fliers provided the 3d Marine Brigade with "reliable information" on the movements of the Chinese, something the other foreign military forces in the area did not have.[18] It is interesting to note that one of Butler's pilots was not a Marine but a young Army Air Corps officer who was temporarily attached to the brigade during June. First Lieutenant Thomas D. White was a military attaché at the American Legation in Peking but had received special permission to join the Marine airmen in their patrol duty. Thirty years later, White became Air Force Chief of Staff.

Later in the summer of 1928, a few more patrols were flown in an area north of Tientsin where Nationalist troops were maneuvering. Nonetheless, General Butler reported in July that he felt the Marine mission in North China was completed. The Nationalist takeover of the north produced no looting of foreign property nor attacks on foreign residents. Inevitably, the question of withdrawing the brigade arose. Beginning in September, Marine planes were relocated to the island of Guam and to the United States. Fighting Plane Squadron 6M moved to Shanghai on the 15th.[19] Two and a half weeks later, it boarded the transport *Henderson* for the trip back to San Diego. At the end of September, the headquarters detachment of the air group was deactivated, leaving only one squadron at Hsin Ho. In the meantime, ground units were being gradually pulled out of North China. Both MacMurray and Butler, however, felt a complete withdrawal from China was unwise at the time and desired the retention of at least a part of the brigade. Admiral Bristol, on the other hand, favored a total pullout of the 3d Brigade. In a running series of correspondence, Minister MacMurray and the admiral presented their views to authorities in Washington. Bristol's argument for the most part was adopted, and the withdrawal of Marines continued, except for the Legation Guard in Peking and the 4th Regiment in Shanghai. The latter remained deployed on a reduced level.

In mid-November, the last Marine aviation unit in China, Observation Squadron 10, began closing down Camp MacMurray and prepared for its return journey to the United States. On the 22nd, all personnel and equipment still at the base were loaded on board the *Chaumont* which sailed first to Shanghai. The ship then left for San Diego a week later. The 3d Marine Brigade eventually was deactivated on 13 January 1929. General Butler and the remaining units pulled out of Tientsin and were redeployed to the United States a short time later.

In the first 12 months of the deployment, Marine planes flew 2,343.2 hours during a total of 3,731 flights. There were five crashes but with no injuries to the crews. During the same period, Marine aviators flying in Nicaragua, although having more time in the air (6,067.5 hours), had fewer flights (3,678). They also sustained seven crashes resulting in one injury and two deaths. From 1 July 1928 until the final departure, Marine airmen in China flew 757.5 hours during 834 flights with no crashes, a unique achievement since crashes occurred in all other localities where Marine planes were assigned.[20] Among the fliers in China were at least seven who would become leaders of Marine aviation in World War II and in the postwar period.[21] The deployment to China provided these airmen and their compatriots with valuable experience in functioning as an integral part of an air-ground expedition, the first in Marine Corps history.

Butler's experience in commanding a combined air-ground force led him to conclude that aviation squadrons:

"... should be a part of the brigade, 'body and soul,' and not a
separate arm directed by and under the control of some officer
in Washington. The idea that no one but an air officer can direct

or control them is erroneous. They are an auxiliary arm, and as such, must not be separated from the command by special regulations which prevent a commander from treating them in the same manner as any other arm."

The well-known activities of Marine aviators in Nicaragua, which occurred simultaneously with the deployment in China, tended to overshadow the air activities in the latter country. As a result, the story of Marine aviators in China and how they got there has been largely forgotten with the passage of time. Few realized that it was only through the vigorous efforts of Brigadier General Smedley D. Butler that aviation squadrons were brought in and then operated as a viable force in China. A good argument can be made that without his continual support and concern, there would have been no aviation contingent in China, or at best such a contingent would not have had a significant role in the expedition. His persistent advocacy of the aviation units before superiors in the Navy and State Departments insured a place for Marine aviation in America's military policy in China. Butler, who had a visionary concept of aviation, felt that these aviation squadrons were "the biggest asset" in the U.S. presence in China.[22] Sometime later, he stated: "I have always believed that had it not been for the splendidly efficient air force attached to the 3d Brigade in China, we could not have avoided bloodshed. The air force was of more value to me than a regiment."[23]

Notes

1. At 16, Butler was commissioned as a second lieutenant in 1898 after lying about his age. He participated in the Spanish-American War, the Philippine Insurrection, and the Boxer Rebellion. Subsequently, he took part in the American interventions in the Caribbean and Central America. During World War I, the veteran campaigner was promoted to brigadier general.
2. John V. A. MacMurray telegram to Secretary of State, 6 April 1927, *Papers Relating to the Foreign Relations of the United States 1927,* Vol. 11 (Washington, D.C.: U.S. Government Printing Office, 1942), pp. 104–105.

3. Muster Rolls, 3d Brigade, April–May 1927: Brigadier General Smed-ley D. Butler letter to Commandant of the Marine Corps, 22 April 1927 and Butler letter to Commandant, 27 April 1927, Personal Papers Collection (PC 54), History and Museums Division, Headquarters Marine Corps.
4. Message from Headquarters Marine Corps (HQMC) to Commander in Chief, Asiatic Fleet, no date, 3d Brigade Records, 1975–70/5–3, Archives Section, History and Museums Division, HQMC; Muster Rolls, 3d Brigade, May 1927.
5. Message to Naval Communications Office, Washington, D.C., 1975–70/5–3 3d Brigade records; Testimony before Subcommittee of House Committee on Appropriations on Navy Department Appropriations Bill for 1929 of Major E. H. Brainard, 70th Congress, 1st Session, p. 703.
6. During the deployment, units of Aircraft Squadrons, 3d Brigade were both reorganized and redesignated. Muster Rolls, 3d Brigade May–June 1927.
7. Butler letter to Colonel Henry C. Davis, Commanding Officer, Provisional Regiment, Olongapo, 4 May 1927, 3d Brigade records 1975–70/5–3.
8. Kenneth W. Condit and Edwin T. Turnbladh, *Hold High the Torch: A History of the 4th Marines,* (Washington, D.C.: Historical Branch, G-3 Division, HQMC, 1960), p. 141; Butler letter to Commandant, 12 May 1927, PC 54; Butler letter to Davis, 30 May 1927, PC 54.
9. Muster Rolls, Aircraft Squadrons, 3d Brigade, June–July 1927; Butler letter to Commandant 16 July 1927, PC 54; Butler letter to Admiral Mark Bristol, 31 December 1928, 3d Brigade records 1975–70/5–3.
10. MacMurray letter to Williams, 16 June 1927, PC 54; Butler letter to Commandant, 31 May 1927, PC 54. Butler letter to Davis, 30 May 1927, PC 54.
11. Butler letter to Commandant, 16 July 1927, PC 54; Lieutenant Colonel Arthur J. Burks, "China Side 1927," *Marine Corps Gazette,* April 1949, p. 50.
12. Jules Archer, *The Plot to Seize the White House* (New York: Hawthorn Books, Inc., 1973), p. 97; Butler letter to Commandant, 2 September 1927, PC 54; Davis letter to Commandant, 30 August 1927, PC 54; Butler letter to Bristol, 31 December 1928, 3d Brigade records 1975–70/5–3.
13. Butler letter to Commandant, 16 July 1927, PC 54; Butler letter to Commandant, 31 May 1927, PC 54; Butler letter to Bristol, 18 November 1927, PC 54; Robert Sherrod, *History of Marine Corps Aviation in World War II* (Washington, D.C.: Combat Forces Press, 1952), p. 28.
14. Butler letter to Commandant, 27 December 1927, PC 54; Major General Francis B. Loomis, USMC (Ret.), Oral History Interview, pp. 39–41, History and Museums Division, HQMC.

15. Muster Rolls, 3d Brigade, January 1928; Butler letter to Commandant 31 January 1928, PC 54; *Papers Relating to the Foreign Relations of the United States 1928,* Vol. II (Washington, D.C.: U.S. Government Printing Office, 1943), p. 309.

16. Final Report of the 3d Marine Brigade, pp. 57–60, 1975–70/5–3.

17. 3d Brigade Diary, Operations and Training, 17 May–10 September 1928; AS 4 Report of Aircraft Squadrons, 3d Brigade, 15–31 October 1928, History and Museums Division, HQMC.

18. Final Report, p. 70, 1975–70/5–3; Butler letter to Bristol, 31 December 1928, p. 12, 1975–70/5–3; Major General John Lejeune, USMC, testimony on Navy Department Appropriation Bill for 1930, 23 January 1929, p. 654; Loomis oral history transcript, pp. 38–39.

19. This unit is the lineal ancestor of present Marine Fighter Attack Squadron 232, one of the oldest squadrons on active duty in the Corps. In World War II, it took part in the defense of Pearl Harbor during the Japanese attack and went on to participate in six more campaigns. In the Indochina War, the squadron had three separate combat tours in Vietnam and one in Thailand. It was one of the last Marine units to leave Southeast Asia.

20. Muster Rolls, 3d Brigade, July 1928–January 1929; Charles Francis Adams, *Report of the Secretary of the Navy 1929* (Washington, D.C.: U.S. Government Printing Office, 1930), pp. 594–595. Curtis D. Wilbur, Report *of the Secretary of the Navy 1928* (Washington, D.C.: U.S. Government Printing Office, 1929), pp. 675–676.

21. Major General Francis B. Loomis, Lieutenant General William J. Wallace, Major General William G. Manley, Lieutenant General Clayton C. Jerome, Major General James T. Moore, General William O. Brice, Major General Walter G. Farrell.

22. Upon his return, General Butler was rewarded with the command of the Marine Base at Quantico, and was promoted to major general in July 1929. Within three years, the general, one of America's most renowned military officers, ended his 33-year career by retiring to private life.

23. Final Report, pp. 102–103, 1975–70/5–3.

Miss Neufeld received her B.A. in history from Molloy College, Rockville Centre, New York, and did her graduate work in Far Eastern History at Georgetown University. Since 1969, she has been employed at Headquarters Marine Corps and is presently Head of the Reference Section, History and Museums Division. She has coauthored articles for various publications.

Mr. Santelli has both a B.A. and a M.A. in history from the University of San Francisco. From 1967–1974, he was a historian in the Marine Corps' Division of History and Museums, and occupied positions in its Reference Section and General Histories Unit. He has coauthored articles on Marine Corps topics that have appeared in various publications. Mr. Santelli is now a writer for the Department of Labor.

2 "The Genesis of Air Support in Guerrilla Operations"

General Vernon E. Megee, USMC (Ret.)

U.S. Naval Institute *Proceedings*
(June 1965): 48–59

Not even its hard-won experience during the long, vicious Haitian Campaign could prepare the U.S. Marine Corps for the five-year Second Nicaraguan Campaign, because Nicaragua was five times the size of Haiti. A new weapon had to be found, and thus it was that the Marine Corps' air-ground team came into being.

THE CURRENTLY REPORTED DIFFICULTIES in providing effective close air support for the Vietnamese forces engaged in guerrilla operations against infiltrating Viet Cong units may strike a responsive chord in the memories of older officers who served under similar conditions in the jungled mountains of Nicaragua from 1927 to 1932. For those younger officers now actually or potentially concerned with so-called counter-insurgency activities, a review of the early development of air support techniques against elusive irregulars may possibly prove to be of more than passing historical interest.

The highly effective system of close air support developed by the Navy-Marine Corps during World War II, and later perfected in Korea, had its genesis in the guerrilla operations of the Marines against Nicaragua's "General" Sandino. In the process of this evolution, however, both equipment and techniques have become less adaptable to guerrilla warfare than they were in the beginning. It is time, perhaps, to review the requirements, with a view toward simplification of the means. Some reorientation in the light of historical perspective might be helpful as a prelude to definite recommendations. Lessons learned during the second Nicaraguan Campaign may well prove valid for Vietnam.

Early in 1927, the civil war then raging in Nicaragua threatened to spread beyond its allotted bounds. The Marines and Bluejackets from the ancient cruisers of the Special Service Squadron who had been monitoring the situation for some months were no longer adequate for the task. The squadron commander, Rear Admiral Latimer, asked for substantial assistance. The hard-pressed Marines responded by calling in the mail guards to reconstitute the Fifth Regiment, which was then dispatched piecemeal to the port of Corinto, the last elements—including the newly appointed brigade commander and his staff—arriving on 7 March. As a supporting element, Marine Observation Squadron One had also been ordered from San Diego, to provide "reconnaissance and communication" missions for the expeditionary brigade.

This first contingent of Marine aviation to be committed, under command of the then Major Ross E. (Rusty) Rowell, arrived in Corinto harbor on 26 February and unloaded its crated airplanes from ship to waiting flat cars for the ride to Managua. There were six DH-4 biplanes, powered by World War I water-cooled Liberty engines, armed with two .30-caliber machine guns and bomb racks for ten 17-pound fragmentation bombs. The top speed of these aircraft did not greatly exceed 100 miles per hour, but their landing speed was correspondingly low. The other planes of the squadron complement were OL-6s, the early model of the Loening amphibian, powered with a single water-cooled engine— the inverted Packard V-12. The author does not recall that these planes carried any armament other than the Scarff-mounted Lewis gun in the observer's cockpit. They were included in the squadron complement in the hope that they would be useful in an undeveloped country of many lakes and rivers. They were most useful indeed!

The only semblance of an airdrome available in the Managua area was an unimproved cow pasture then in use by the "Nicaraguan Air Force"—a quasi-military organization consisting solely of two Laird-Swallow biplanes powered by Curtiss OX5 engines, and two North American pilots, Brooks and Mason. Since they must be credited with the first efforts toward air support in the Nicaraguan campaign, these two escaped characters from the pages of a Richard Harding Davis novel deserve at least brief mention.

During the battle of Chinandega, fought during early February between the Liberal (insurrectionist) and the Conservative (government) forces, a savage encounter which virtually destroyed the town and caused the deaths of hundreds of Nicaraguans, most of them non-combatants including women and children, Brooks and Mason had participated to the extent of flying over the area and dropping a few handmade dynamite "bombs"—the short fuses of which were allegedly lighted from their cigars. While these missiles were undoubtedly more terrifying than lethal, the effect was to stampede the Liberal soldiers and give the victory to the Conservative forces, which up until then had not been doing too well for themselves. The discomfited Liberal leaders promptly castigated the "American aviators" for their inhumane conduct of war and the massacre of the innocents. While it appears very unlikely, considering the inadequacy of their equipment, that these mercenary aviators actually caused many casualties, the morale effect on the rebel soldiers and the terrified townsmen alike was considerable. The resultant hue and cry in the press also proved embarrassing to the American Minister. Messrs. Brooks and Mason were shortly thereafter quietly retired from the scene, leaving to the Marine aviators who succeeded them a rather unsavory polemical heritage, and two decrepit Laird-Swallow biplanes.

Major Rowell commandeered the Nicaraguan "airdrome" and assembled his aircraft as quickly as possible. While this task required but a few days, it must be pointed out that expeditionary aircraft should arrive at the scene in flying condition; modern guerrilla warfare would not usually permit such a leisurely approach to combat readiness.

The first combat mission of record for the newly arrived Marine squadron was flown on 18 March, when two of the DH-4s reported the progress of the battle of Muy Muy, remaining scrupulously aloof from the hostilities—not so the ubiquitous Brooks and Mason, flying their last mission in the service of the Nicaraguan government. In their colorful action report (to *The New York Times*), they complained that their wheezing engines would barely clear the intervening mile-high pass at Boaca, that their ammonia and dynamite bombs failed to explode, and that they suffered severe damage to their aircraft from small arms fire. In fact, they were barely able to flutter back to an emergency airstrip in deferred forced landings. The insurgents appeared to have learned much since Chinandega, and were able to drive the Conservatives from the field despite their air support.

On 28 March, at Leon on the Managua-Corinto railroad, Marines and Nicaraguans clashed briefly in an innocuous exchange of shots; and one of the Marine observation planes was hit by small arms fire while passing over Dario. The next day an armed DH-4, patrolling the rail line near Leon was hit 12 times (presumably by a machine gun burst). The pilot, Captain H. D. (Spud) Campbell, notwithstanding his aircraft's damaged control surfaces, immediately dove on his assailants and scattered them with machine gun fire. These two brief actions marked the end of the neutral observation phase and the beginning of actual U.S. military participation in the Nicaraguan civil war.

There followed a lull in hostilities while the Stimson Commission sought a truce between the opposing factions. As a result of the conference of Tipitapa, the insurgent leaders, save one, agreed to turn in their arms—for a price. Mr. Henry L. Stimson somewhat prematurely reported to Washington that the civil war in Nicaragua had definitely ended and that bloodshed had ceased. The skeptical Marines settled down to watchful waiting; the aviators continued sporadic patrolling.

Mr. Stimson's message hardly could have cleared the decoding desk in the Department of State when the Navy Department received news of more ominous import. All was *not* well in Nicaragua. American blood had been spilled there once again. The emphasis now passed from the realm of the diplomats into the hands of the military. Once again the U.S. Marine Corps found itself engaged in tropical guerrilla warfare, which in scale, duration, and ferocity was to test severely its mettle and endurance.

The triggering event was a night encounter in the village of La Paz Centro between some 300 armed insurgents under one "General" Cabulla, and a Marine detachment under Captain R. B. Buchanan. In the confused street fighting which followed, Captain Buchanan and one other Marine were killed, two wounded. Fourteen dead bandits were left in the streets, and an indeterminate number of wounded escaped. The Marines held the town against heavy numerical odds, thanks to superior discipline and marksmanship. This was, of course, accomplished without air support. Marine aviators of the period were not qualified for night flying, nor did there exist the requisite communication gear for such support. It would never have occurred to Captain Buchanan, or any contemporary ground commander, to expect any aerial assistance under such circumstances.

In the ensuing weeks, the Marines deployed into the mountainous interior of northern Nicaragua, prodded into this aggressive action by the depredations of "General" Augusto Sandino, the insurgent leader who had refused to abide by the truce of Tipitapa, and subsequently had taken to the brush with an estimated 200 armed followers. The Marine aviators had attempted to cover his movements, without notable success. The jungle trails often withheld their secrets from aerial observers.

The aviators did, however, maintain contact with the small Marine patrols and isolated village garrisons through daily reconnaissance and liaison flights. The ground Marines co-operated by clearing emergency airstrips near the principal garrison towns, appreciating in their isolation this periodic aerial contact with Managua.

Since the aircraft of 1927 carried no radio equipment, and the ground forces had only cumbersome and unreliable signal sets, the problem of air-ground communication proved acute. Experiment toward solution included cloth panels laid out on the ground in coded arrangement, to be answered by the airmen with wing and engine signals. An ingenious method of message pick-up was perfected, wherein the pilot attempted to hook a trailing weighted line over a pole-suspended message bag. The airmen could also, of course, communicate by dropping a message stick. None of these means was very effective, however, in rough, wooded country. All required the aircraft to remain in very close proximity to the contacted ground unit, thus tending to advertise its presence and progress to all concerned. There were, for this reason, patrol leaders who deliberately avoided seeking contact with searching aircraft. On the other hand, there were those who invariably signaled for a message pick-up, on whatever pretext, whether or not their need had military validity. For instance, there was the major of the old school—with a perennial thirst— who requested, and received, his daily dropped ration of ice. Another patrol leader requested an emergency landing on a marginal airstrip in order to acquaint the somewhat unsympathetic aviator with the current shortage of toilet paper in his camp.

Despite these often amusing frustrations and misunderstandings as to the proper role of supporting aviation, this short period of deployment strengthened the bond between air and ground, resulting in at least a partial appreciation of each others' problems. The usefulness of aviation in reconnaissance, liaison, and for emergency transportation had been demonstrated and accepted; few ground commanders, however, were ready to admit that the air arm was capable of effective combat support. Notwithstanding the prior employment of Marine air units in the post war occupation of Haiti and San Domingo, there had been no opportunity—save for a very few single plane engagements—to demonstrate ground attack capability.

This prevalent skepticism was to be dramatically reversed on 16 July at Ocotal, a mountain town on the upper Coco River. Captain Gilbert D. Hatfield, with a mixed force of 37 Marines and 47 Nicaraguan *guardia* had but recently established a garrison within the town. Sandino was known to be in the general vicinity but was believed to have only a few followers. No one took him to be a serious threat—least of all, Captain Hatfield, who in fact had amused himself by exchanging insulting messages with the bandit leader. Sandino, thus taunted, defied the Marines to come and get him; on second thought, he decided to go get the Marines. With a force later estimated to consist of 500 or 600 men, Sandino moved swiftly on the heels of his last defiant message, and during the early evening hours of 15 July, completed his stealthy approach on Ocotal. Although Captain Hatfield was not expecting an attack, he was not—in the military sense of the word—surprised; an alert sentry detected the approach of armed men and fired the warning shots which brought the sleeping garrison to arms. Protected by the thick masonry walls of their separate billets, the Marines and *guardia* were able to stand off the attackers until morning. Sandino then suspended the attack while he regrouped his forces and demanded Hatfield's surrender. The reply delivered to the bearers of the flag of truce may have been somewhat deficient in terms of old world courtesy but left no doubt in Sandino's mind as to Hatfield's intention. The battle was rejoined.

At 1000, there appeared over the town a two-plane reconnaissance patrol flown by Lieutenant Hayne Boyden and Marine Gunner "Mike" Wodarcyzk, a redoubtable and colorful pair of aviators. Somehow sensing trouble, Lieutenant Boyden landed on the adjacent airstrip while Wodarcyzk covered him from the air. Excited natives gave Boyden some inkling of the true situation, and he immediately took off under scattered rifle fire. He rejoined his wingman, and the two of them expended their ammunition on strafing runs against the bandit positions before returning full throttle for Managua to sound the alarm. Up until this time, Captain Hatfield had been unable to communicate with brigade headquarters. The returning aviators reached the base airdrome at 1215.

Within the hour, the five available DH-4 airplanes had been armed with light fragmentation bombs and full belts of machine gun ammunition.

Major Rowell, the squadron commander, led the flight off the 400 yards of turf runway, across Lake Managua and over the 5,000-foot mountain chain to Ocotal (no small feat in itself during any afternoon of the Nicaraguan rainy season). By 1500, the flight was over Ocotal, circling at 1,500 feet above the town, and receiving small arms fire. Major Rowell later reported:

> I led off the attack and dived out of column from 1,500 feet, pulling out at about 600. Later we ended up by diving in from 1,000 and pulling out at 300. Since the enemy had not been subjected to any form of bombing attack, other than the dynamite charges thrown from the Laird-Swallows by the Nicaraguan Air Force, they had no fear of us. They exposed themselves in such a manner that we were able to inflict damage which was out of proportion to what they might have suffered had they taken cover.

The *jefe politico* of Ocotal, who was an eye witness of the air attack, also contributed his version to history:

> At 10:00 a.m. two planes are seen flying low. . . . they fire on Sandino's forces and leave.
> . . . At 3:00 p.m. five planes appear in battle formation, form line and open fire with their ten machine guns. . . . They drop bombs on Sandino's army, now beginning to retreat
> . . . 5:00 p.m., all quiet.

This air action, generally recognized to be the first organized dive bombing and low altitude attack ever made in direct support of ground troops, was decisive. Sandino and the survivors of his force fled, leaving an estimated 40 to 80 dead behind him, with probably at least twice as many wounded. The fire fight at Ocotal had lasted altogether more than 16 hours; had it not been for the protection provided by the thick-walled houses, the Marines and *guardia* could hardly have survived the night. While their total casualties were light, they were actually in a desperate plight with but little ammunition left when Rowell's flight arrived. Certainly Major Rowell was justified in reporting that Marine aviation "had saved the garrison from great loss of life and almost certain destruction."

The attacking planes were hit repeatedly by small arms fire from the ground—Major Rowell reported 44 bullet holes in his aircraft—but fortunately all escaped serious damage and were able to return to Managua. This demonstrated resistance to battle damage gave the aviators greater confidence in their machines, and undoubtedly encouraged more reckless exposure in subsequent encounters.

The battle of Ocotal established Marine aviation as a full-fledged partner in what was later to become famous as the Marine air-ground team. The outstanding success of Rowell's small flight was particularly remarkable in that it was accomplished by long-obsolete aircraft with grossly inadequate armament.

Following the Ocotal engagement, brigade headquarters despatched Major Oliver Floyd with a force of 100 Marines and *guardia* in hot pursuit of Sandino's fleeing band. Major Floyd was supported by reconnaissance flights, which repeatedly reported concentrations of bandits on Chipote, near Quílali, and in the vicinity of Telepanaca, Jícaro, and other places southeast of Ocotal. Notwithstanding these warnings which were dropped to Floyd's patrol, small bands of *sandinistas* ambushed the Marine column on two occasions, but were driven off without much difficulty. Major Floyd completed his patrol without encountering any major armed bands, which led him to report that "the country was deserted—inhabitants probably in hiding." This purely negative report was at variance with the air intelligence on file at brigade headquarters, but was nevertheless accepted at Managua as indicative of Sandino's complete defeat—a most unfortunate conclusion.

By early August, those in authority had become convinced that Sandino's revolt had been quelled. The Marine expeditionary force was reduced to some 1,300 men and garrisons redistributed accordingly. Barely enough men were left in the northern area to hold the principal towns and patrol their supply lines; further offensive action was considered impracticable.

Meanwhile, Sandino had gained a host of sympathizers and had been able to assemble a well-armed force of possibly 1,000 men. He could now bring superior numbers against the attenuated Marine forces at whatever point he chose. During late August and September, there occurred numerous attacks on Marine garrisons, and harassing ambushes against the under strength patrols and supply trains. Air support of these units was drastically restricted due to the inclement weather conditions prevalent during the rainy season.

Early in October, Sandino was given the opportunity to strike back at the Marine aviators who had been his nemesis at Ocotal. Although the aviators as yet had suffered no fatalities from enemy fire, so frequently encountered, their luck suddenly ran out. On 8 October a two-plane patrol discovered and attacked a bandit concentration of some 200 men near Sapotillal Ridge, killing "many" and dispersing the rest. Shortly thereafter, one of the planes, apparently hit, was observed to make a crash landing on the side of a brush-covered hill. The pilot, Lieutenant E. A. Thomas, and his enlisted observer, Sergeant Dowdell, were seen to run away from the wreckage shortly before it burst into flame. They were never sighted alive after that, but their misfortune touched off a series of sanguinary encounters as the Marine ground forces made heroic efforts to rescue their aerial brethren. Marine aviation at that time did not afford the luxury of an air rescue service—rotary wing aircraft being yet some distance into the future.

A mixed patrol of 40 Marines and *guardia*, under Lieutenant George O'Shea, set out from Jícaro on October 9 to search for the missing aviators. Some hours later, while approaching the vicinity of the crash, they were ambushed by a large force of well-armed bandits. After a desperate fight which lasted over two hours, the patrol managed to extricate itself under cover of darkness and returned with difficulty to Jícaro. The mission could not have succeeded in any event. Thomas and Dowdell were dead blasted out of a cave with dynamite bombs and cut to pieces with machetes.

A second attempt at rescue met with similar misfortune on 27 October, six miles southeast of Jícaro. Lieutenant C. J. Chappell and his patrol of 35 men were ambushed by a force of some 250 *sandinistas*, who, fortunately, were not so valorous as they had been in the O'Shea fight. Lieutenant Chappell was supported by an air patrol (which attacked the bandit positions as directed by ground panel signals), and was re-enforced at the critical moment by Lieutenant Moses Gould and his detachment of mounted Marines. The attackers were driven off after 35 minutes of sharp fighting, only to return later in the day for a second repulse.

The valiant efforts at rescue by these ground patrols, although unsuccessful, cancelled out the debt owed the flying Marines for the Ocotal rescue, and cemented the beginning of that air-ground co-ordination which was to develop many years later into such a lethal combination against the Japanese and, still later, the North Koreans.

The Marine aviators, meanwhile, had continued their aggressive patrolling of the bandit-infested areas, and had confirmed persistent intelligence reports that Sandino's main force of several hundred men was concentrating on a strongly fortified hill in eastern Nueva Segovia. A stepped up bombing offensive was planned; legitimate travelers were warned to stay out of the area. Before any effective air attacks could be executed, however, the skeletonized ground forces suffered further disasters.

On 19 December, Captain Richard Livingston left Jinotega for Nueva Segovia with a detachment of 115 Marine replacements, accompanied by a pack train of over 200 animals and the attendant *muleros*. The trail chosen led through wild and rugged country, largely unfamiliar to Livingston or his subordinates. A second detachment of some 60 Marines and *guardia* under Lieutenant M. A. Richal, marched eastward from Pueblo Nuevo with orders to join Livingston at Quílali.

Ten days after its departure from Jinotega, while approaching Quílali through a narrow defile, Livingston's ungainly column was effectively ambushed by a large group of bandits. In the ensuing melee, five Marines and one *guardia* were killed, 25 wounded (including Livingston and Gould), and the pack train was stampeded, taking with it supplies and reserve ammunition. Lieutenant Gould managed to extricate the column from the defile and deploy it for battle on more open ground. The bandits were finally driven off, with the assistance of an attacking air patrol which fortuitously appeared on the scene, but the Marines were largely immobilized and in no position to claim the victory.

Later the same day (30 December), Richal's column was also ambushed while yet several miles west of Quílali. The initial assault was repulsed with only one Marine wounded, but the bandits continued sporadic attacks on the bivouac during the night. The next day Lieutenant Richal was again ambushed by a force of some 400 bandits. The ensuing fight lasted over an hour before the bandits withdrew leaving 30 dead behind them. They also left behind them a much battered Marine patrol, Lieutenant Richal seriously wounded, Bruce (the *guardia* commander) dead, three others seriously wounded. Gunnery Sergeant Brown assumed command, dug in along a ridge and awaited relief. The next day a relief column, supported by an air patrol, managed to extricate Richal's column and return with it to Quílali. Thus was the planned junction of Livingston and Richal effected—but hardly according to plan.

The immediate problem was the evacuation of the 30 wounded men, which included the two commanders and the medical officer. Air evacuation was the only possibility, but there was no airstrip at Quílali. The surviving Marines improvised a marginal strip 250 yards long by demolishing all the flimsy buildings along one side of Quílali's deserted main street. Lieutenant Christian F. (Frank) Schilt volunteered for the evacuation mission. Flying a newly arrived Vought O2U Corsair biplane, fitted with oversize landing gear but no brakes, Lieutenant Schilt made repeated flights into Quílali during the period 6 to 8 January 1928, all under enemy fire. His landings had to be slowed by Marines dragging on the wings; his take-offs were "catapulted" by Marines holding the plane in position until the engine was developing full power. That all flights were completed safely was nothing short of miraculous. For this feat of "almost superhuman skill," Lieutenant Schilt was awarded the Congressional Medal of Honor for valor "beyond the call of duty." Both ground and air Marines were agreed that never was a decoration more fully deserved.

A combined ground and air attack against Sandino's fortified stronghold on Chipote Mountain was now planned for 14 January. In the event, the ground element, under Major A. Young, ran into a strong outpost position and lost considerable time. The aviators went ahead with the planned bombing and strafing attacks, inflicting considerable damage to the fortifications and reporting heavy casualties to bandit personnel. Major Young's advance on the ground was further slowed by his methodical insistence on blocking all escape routes before making his final attack. When he arrived, on 26 January, 12 days after the air attack, the bird had flown. The elusive Sandino had triumphed once again.

This apparent lack of co-ordination between air and ground units may be largely, but not entirely, attributed to faulty communications. The planes were still without radio, and for days would be unable to contact ground patrols on heavily jungled trails. Nevertheless, there lingers the suspicion that the aviators were too impatient to get on with the deferred attack on Chipote, and that no one on the brigade staff felt sufficiently informed to insist on a coordinated attack.

By the end of January, it was conceded that Sandino had an organized force of about 1,500 armed men operating in northern Nicaragua. The Eleventh Regiment of Marines was now ordered to take over the Northern Area. The movement of the regiment and its supplies by bull cart and pack train, with token assistance from the two Fokker transport planes but recently arrived, consumed more than a month. Aviation covered the movement with daily reconnaissance patrols.

An additional aviation squadron, including three more transport aircraft, was now added to the brigade; landing strips were improved throughout the area. The obsolete DH-4 airplanes were being replaced by O2U's and the new Curtiss Falcon attack aircraft. The new planes came equipped with air-cooled engines of somewhat greater power and reliability, and were capable of carrying heavier bomb loads. The original 17-pound bombs gave way to 30-pounders and 50-pounders; later to 100-pounders. However, effective means of air ground communication were still lacking; the new planes did not carry radio equipment. The original squadron organization now became in effect an air group, and had meanwhile moved to a larger and better equipped airdrome. The main turf runway was now some 2,000 feet long with clear approaches, ample distance for even the tri-motored Fokkers. Shops and hangars were built, barracks replaced tents, and the Marine air base gradually assumed an air of semi-permanence. Lacking, of course, were any aids to navigation, or lights for night flying. All flying was by contact point-to-point navigation, using such inaccurate maps as existed. The occasional pilot who returned home after dark had to land by flickering oil flares, sometimes using as a reference point the white horse which habitually grazed on the field.

There were numerous bandit contacts during the rest of 1928. The air arm continued to support these ground actions where possible, hampered still by lack of adequate communications. On 19 March, the flyers found and routed a big Sandino force caught for once in open country, inflicting severe casualties during repeated attacks. An air observer, Captain F. E. Pierce, was wounded in the foot; a bullet lodged in his pilot's parachute pack; and other planes in the flight were hit. All returned safely to Managua. After that episode, armor plate was fitted under the seats of all aircraft.

In early May, a detachment of amphibious planes was established at Puerto Cabezas, on the east coast of Nicaragua, to support better the planned river operations in that area. These were OL-8s, carrying armament, with room in the capacious hull for two extra passengers or equivalent air freight. A better aircraft for the purpose did not exist, a combination observation, attack, and transport design never at a loss for a place to land. The "ducks," as they were inevitably to be called, proved invaluable to Merritt A. "Red Mike" Edson during his famous Coco River patrol, as well as to other patrol commanders operating in the Eastern Area; they must be given credit for materially assisting in the blunting of Sandino's thrusts into that area.

By the end of 1928, the co-ordination between air and ground units had greatly improved with practice. The new types of aircraft had removed some of the hazards from jungle flying, and the aviators were extending their patrols to the most remote areas of Nicaragua. Particularly noteworthy was the employment of the Fokker transports (later replaced by Fords) on scheduled runs between Managua and Ocotal, which greatly facilitated movement of personnel to and from the combat zone, evacuation of the wounded, and the supply of critical items to the troops.

The year 1929 was a quiet one in Nicaragua, a period of transition from Marine to *guardia* control. Marine aviation continued the routine support of both forces, with but little diversion in the way of hostile contacts. The troops in the field were now habitually paid by air-dropped money bags—none of which was ever lost. A regular air freight department had been organized at Managua for preparation of these dropped deliveries to the more remote outposts, ranging from bundles of newspapers to special orders of outsize shoes. The observers soon developed unerring skill with these missiles, seldom missing the bullseye of the dropping ground. There is record of one Marine being struck by a bean bag, and of one bull succumbing to a direct hit from a bundle of *The New York Times*.

In June 1930, the aviators had their last chance at Sandino, trapped on Saraguasca Mountain on one of his forays toward the coffee district of Jinotega. As at Ocotal, the first contact was made by a returning two-plane patrol which responded to signals for assistance from an outnumbered *guardia* unit. Lieutenants Byron Johnson and Jesse Young were the pilots who launched the initial air attack, which caught the bandits in fairly open country on top of the mountain and did them considerable damage while ammunition lasted. The follow-up attack, launched in the afternoon, consisted of five planes led by Major Ralph Mitchell, the then air group commander. By this time, however, the bandits had taken cover, leaving only an area target for the aviators, which was thoroughly bombed and strafed but with results unknown. Sandino, wounded in the leg by a bomb fragment, escaped the encircling *guardia* patrols under cover of darkness and disappeared into the jungle fastness of Nueva Segovia. The aviators felt that the *guardia* should have moved faster, but again the lack of communication hindered air-ground co-ordination.

During early 1931, the Marines were withdrawn from the outlying districts and concentrated in Managua, Matagalpa, and Ocotal, where they continued to act as a reserve for the *guardia* units which had taken over the active patrolling. There was but little further action by the Marine ground forces pending their withdrawal at the end of 1932. On the other hand, the aviation element of the Marine brigade continued all-out support of *guardia* activities until the end of the occupation. There were numerous contacts of record during this later period, and one plane was lost to hostile ground fire during an attack on bandits at Siclin, in the Eastern Area, on 23 July 1931. The pilot executed a deferred forced landing, burned his plane, and, with his observer, made good his escape after an odyssey of some 40 swampy miles and several days elapsed time—probably the pioneer example of escape and evasion.

It is worthy of note that only two Marine aircraft were actually shot down by ground fire during the five years of guerrilla operation in Nicaragua, although some of them returned to base literally sieved with bullet holes. Only two aviators were killed and one wounded by direct enemy action; operational accidents due to weather and other causes took a much higher toll.

In summary, the accomplishments of our small supporting air force in Nicaragua contributed materially to the efforts of the Marine brigade. There are those who believed that the Marines could not have restored law and order to turbulent Nicaragua, nor have maintained sizeable ground forces in the roadless mountain jungle of Nueva Segovia province without the aid of their air arm. Sandino enjoyed superior mobility on his own ground; he could concentrate superior forces at the point of contact. Only the air patrols could really hamper his movements, forcing him to travel at night or during inclement weather. Only aerial reconnaissance could detect the presence of large concentrations of bandits in such an area—even the air arm on occasion was unable to maintain surveillance of the wily enemy, who learned after Ocotal the art of cover and camouflage. Only the air arm could concentrate heavy weapons on a given target; the Marines had no artillery. And finally, it was aerial transport which linked the outposts with the rail head at Managua and gave to the isolated garrisons and patrols a flexibility of operation which would have been impossible with bull cart and pack transportation. There was also the morale factor, definitely present but always difficult to assess, of knowing that friendly air cover was never very far away.

Marine aviation performed its various missions with a true economy of force. Only on three occasions, Ocotal, Chipote, and Saraguasca, could we boast of a concentration of as many as five combat aircraft—on each of these days that number represented the current availability list. The total aircraft strength of the group rarely exceeded 20, including transports and amphibians. The daily combat and reconnaissance patrols consisted of two aircraft allotted to each combat zone; the transport schedule varied according to load backlog. Major and minor maintenance problems with the comparatively simple and sturdy air frames and engines were well within the capabilities of the skilled technicians available at the base airdrome. The group muster roll contained fewer names than would be found on that of a modern squadron operating under group control.

It may be said that Marine aviation came of age during the Nicaraguan campaign. The lessons learned were incorporated in the training manuals later concocted for the guidance of a younger generation; the officers and men who flew in Nicaragua were destined to be leaders in the great Pacific war; the doctrine of close air support was refined to an exact science through the medium of instant and reliable radio communication; new and far more effective aircraft were made available under the impetus of all-out war to meet better the conditions of major amphibious operations. All this spilled over, of course, into the subsequent Korean hostilities.

Since then, however, the newer types of aircraft have become increasingly less adaptable to the conditions of small-scale guerrilla activities, demanding long, hard-surface runways and excessive air space for their high speed maneuvering. The existing system of arrested landings and accelerated take-offs requires elaborate field gear which may not be available or operable in jungle country. Rotary wing aircraft are too vulnerable to ground fire. Perhaps the new VTOL convertible type of aircraft will be the answer. In any event, the ideal aircraft for the close support of troops in guerrilla operations will be a specialized type, light, durable, highly maneuverable, with speed a secondary consideration, operable from turf runways, with versatile armament. *Such an aircraft need not be particularly useful for any other purpose.* Surely our aircraft industry can meet this challenge.

Aviation squadrons, especially equipped and trained for guerrilla counter-insurgency, should be self-contained and capable of independent actions in the field. They are not so under current organization, being tied to the apron strings of the parent group. Their ground equipment should be streamlined on an austere basis, capable of operation in a largely roadless country. Supported ground forces should be expected to provide for local security and supply of common items. Counter air operations and area air defense should be provided by other, more appropriately equipped, air units, preferably by carrier-based naval and Marine squadrons. The specialized ground support squadrons, to be really effective, must forego the lure of the wild blue yonder; the lower they fly on their support missions in jungle country the longer they will live.

What we need for a close support aircraft, then, is a modern version of what served us so well in Nicaragua. A tool that proved useful 35 years ago would not necessarily be less useful today. We believe in aeronautical progress but, in this case, our aircraft designers and tacticians could do worse than turn to history for their inspiration.

General Megee enlisted in the Marine Corps in 1919 and was commissioned in 1922. His expeditionary duty during the 1920s included Haiti (1923 to 1925), China (1926 to 1928) and Nicaragua (1929 to 1931). During World War II, he served as Chief of Staff, Third Air Wing, and as Commander, Marine Air Support Control Units. He commanded the first Marine Air Wing in Korea throughout 1953. He was Deputy Commander of Fleet Marine Forces, Pacific, and, subsequently, of FMF, Atlantic, prior to becoming Assistant Commandant and Chief of Staff, Marine Corps Headquarters from January 1956 until November 1957. At the time of his retirement in November 1959, he commanded FMF, Pacific. The author of numerous articles, General Megee is co-author of the Marine Corps' *Small Wars Manual* and *Manual for Landing Operations.*

"Ace in a Day"

3

*Lieutenant Commander
Thomas J. Cutler, USN (Ret.)*

U.S. Naval Institute *Proceedings*
(July 2008): 93

IN OCTOBER 1942, the Americans on Guadalcanal were in a fight for their lives. Henderson Field was riddled with bomb craters, wrecked U.S. aircraft were strewn about, and luxuriant jungle vegetation had been replaced by broken trunks protruding from a tangle of charred undergrowth. The nightly shelling from Japanese warships was so severe that some of the pilots chose to sleep in jungle positions near the infantry's front lines to increase their odds of survival.

Marine Captain Joe Foss arrived at this chaotic scene on 9 October to assume duties as executive officer of fighter squadron VMF-121. Immediately upon joining the fray on the 13th, he got his first kill but was soon pounced on by three Zeros. Barely escaping, he landed back at the field with an aircraft full of bullet holes and leaking oil like a sieve. The near-death encounter had its effect as he was heard to say, "You can call me 'Swivel-Neck Joe' from now on."

Undaunted, however, the very next day he got his second kill while nursing a bad engine, and a few days later he bagged three more in a wild melee. He had been in the war zone for a total of nine days and with the requisite five kills, he was already an ace.

This was just the beginning, however. In the days that followed, he continued to make the skies a very hazardous place for enemy aircraft. By the 23rd he had downed 11 Japanese aircraft. His aggressive, close-in tactics, which caused another pilot to joke that he often left powder burns on his targets, were not without their cost. In those 11 days, four F4F Wildcats piloted by Foss were too damaged to fly again.

On the 25th, the Japanese launched an all-out air assault on Henderson as part of a concerted effort to overrun the field. Foss and five other Wildcat pilots took to the air at about 1000, quickly shooting down three aircraft—two were Foss's kills. That afternoon he shot down three more to become the Marine Corps' first "ace in a day."

In the off hours when he was not flying, Foss and some of the other fliers took to the jungle, armed with rifles, to hunt for Japanese soldiers. While this kind of aggressiveness was laudable, it was soon forbidden by higher authority because the pilots were considered too valuable to risk in this way.

Foss continued to fight like a tiger in the air, narrowly escaping death on numerous occasions, including ditching once in the ocean, nearly drowning and being consumed by sharks in the process. While Japanese aviators could not subdue this intrepid flier, a much smaller aerial combatant was able to take him out of the skies; Foss fell victim to malaria and had to spend six weeks recuperating in New Caledonia and Australia.

When he returned to the fight in January, he soon shot down more aircraft, bringing his total to 26 kills—a Marine Corps record.

Home from the war with a Medal of Honor among many other decorations, Joe Foss continued to do extraordinary things. Twice elected governor of South Dakota, he also served as first commissioner of the American Football League and was instrumental in the formation of the South Dakota Air National Guard. Joe Foss passed away on New Year's Day 2003.

Lieutenant Commander Cutler is the author of several books, including *A Sailor's History of the U.S. Navy* and *Brown Water, Black Berets.*

4 "Marine Corps Aviation—An Infantryman's Opinion"

Major J. N. Rentz, USMCR

U.S. Naval Institute *Proceedings*
(November 1949): 1277–79

ALONG WITH SPECULATION on discussions at the Key West Conference, a new, a fertile field for inter-Service wrangling opened. As a result, reams and reams of paper will be wasted by proponents of Naval Aviation, Marine Corps Aviation, or a single Service Air Force; yet few if any writers will mention, or even take into consideration the real—the down to earth—reason for aviation as a weapon. An honest appraisal of Marine Corps Aviation and its position in our future military establishment therefore becomes essential.

Talk as they will, the primary reason for the aviator's existence—other than strategic bombing—is support of the infantry, "the Queen of Battles." Since the day an air service was conceived in the womb of the Army Signal Corps, its basic *raison d'être* has been ultimate support of the soldier fighting on land. Support of ships at sea followed as night follows the day. As a consequence America has developed the strongest single *support* weapon the world has seen since Hannibal introduced the elephant.

Before discussing any subject, a student must acquaint himself with the historical background thereof.

Marine Corps Aviation was born on May 22, 1912, when First Lieutenant Alfred Austell Cunningham reported for duty as a student at the
Navy's flight school in Annapolis. Throughout the next few years of its
existence, Marine Air underwent growing pains, acquiring techniques,
mechanical skills and "know-how" of flying as more and more Marines
became interested in the antiquated planes of aviation's early days. World
War I gave added impetus to the flight program.

The period of the '20's and '30's marked the development of a mission which became, in World War II, a hallmark of Marine Corps Aviation. In October, 1919, Lieutenant Lawson H. M. Sanderson, attached to
the Fourth Marine Air Squadron, then flying support missions for Marine
ground units operating against Haitian bandits, conducted the first successful experiments in dive bombing under actual combat conditions.
From that time until the day of Pearl Harbor, Marine Air Squadrons
continued development of the doctrine of close air support, practicing it
in Santo Domingo, China, Nicaragua, and in the islands of the Pacific.

Low budgets and disinterestedness obstructed maturation of Marine
Air during the decades of peace. Congress, generally reluctant to invest in
military preparedness, failed to provide funds for aeronautical expansion
and research. Meanwhile, most American strategists, lacking an appreciation for the potentialities of the new weapon, relegated aviation to a
position of relative unimportance. Thus any progress made by one or
another of the air services was in the field of actual combat experience,
and this advantage was attained by Marine Corps Aviation alone.

In 1931 units of the Marine air arm were assigned to duty with carriers of the Fleet, and for the three years following the flight decks of
the *Langley, Saratoga,* and *Lexington* hummed with activity of Marines
gaining experience at carrier landings and take-offs. By December 7, 1941,
therefore, as far as combat experience was concerned, Marine Corps
Aviation might have been more fully prepared for combat than any other
American air service.

Official recognition and designation of Marine Corps Aviation's wartime missions was made in 1935 when the Navy adopted the Marine Corps Schools' *Tentative Landing Operations Manual*. This publication, and its 1938 replacement, *FTP-167,* spelled out the Marine air arm's role to include, among other things, progressive relief of Naval aviation supporting a landing operation as well as attack in support of ground operations.

From this directive the Marine Corps drew the concept which became the basic function of its aviation branch in World War II, and which, to all intents and purposes, will be its assignment in any future struggle; that is, support of the Fleet Marine Force in amphibious operations. Although Marine pilots, having received their initial training in Naval flight schools, are designated Naval Aviators—fully trained to conduct a purely Naval mission as such—the primary mission of Marine Corps Aviation remains. To execute this assignment it is first necessary to clear the skies of enemy aircraft, then to conduct strafing and close-in bombing attacks when and where requested by Marines on the ground.

In carrying out this duty, Marine flyers frequently operate from aircraft carriers during the initial stages of a landing operation, for adequate shore facilities are not always available. By developing this specialty Marine Air duplicates an activity of Naval aviation, but it is a specialty that cannot be performed by the Air Forces, untrained in carrier landings and unappreciative of naval dispositions, formations, and tactics. On the other hand, Marine pilots are specialists in close-in air support, a tactic discovered and developed by them and later studied and adopted by the Army Air Corps whose Attack Aviation amply demonstrated its practicability. Although duplication of a function again appears to have resulted, close analysis will reveal that Marine aviators place emphasis on air-ground coordination, particularly during the critical ship-to-shore phase of a landing attack. Since the U.S. Air Force is not vitally interested in this type of operation—currently emphasizing training in air-to-air support and strategic bombing, instead—it therefore remains for Marine Corps

Aviation to execute this important function. Furthermore, the specialist training of Marine pilots enables them to perfect the tactical relationship between naval components and Marine ground and air units.

Without bothering to look at the record hung up by Marine Corps Aviation during World War II—it speaks for itself—let us delve into the basis of close-in air support. Just what is it? What does it mean? What is expected of it? What can it do?

Close-in air support is a Marine Corps development. In its accepted military sense it implies immediate and specific assistance by aircraft to infantry units engaged in direct combat with the enemy. This activity is indicative of the objective team-work characteristic of Marines. In this sense, Marines consider aircraft as simply one weapon, along with tanks, artillery, and infantry, made available by the American people to military commanders for the execution of their missions. This concept indicates, moreover, the employment of aircraft in any manner which may be of direct assistance to ground forces, whether engaged in infantry combat ashore or approaching a beach in landing-craft.

As defined by Marine Corps Schools, close-in air support is the *Attack by aircraft of hostile ground targets which are at such close range to friendly front lines as to require detailed integration of each air mission with the fire and movement of the ground forces in order to insure safety, prevent interference with other elements of the combined arms, and permit prompt exploitation of the shock, casualty, and neutralization effect of the air attack.* This doctrine, of course, while it recognizes the necessity and significance of strategic bombing and interdictory attacks, by its very definition excludes all air missions performed outside the range of ground forces. In amplification it may be pointed out that close-in air support is the attack of ground objectives by aircraft employing any or all available agents—bombs, machine guns, smoke, rockets, etc.—within as little as 200 yards of front line troops.

Ground forces, faced with stubborn enemy resistance based on terrain unapproachable by tanks and immune from the effects of artillery or naval gunfire, call for close-in air support. An air attack conducted on such a target must necessarily be tactically integrated with the ground effort in order that the great shock effect of close-in bombing and strafing may be properly exploited. Without thorough training and a complete understanding of the tactics employed by the ground units, as well as perfect liaison between pilots and supported infantry unit commanders, accomplishment of this delicate task becomes well-nigh impossible. It is likewise essential for the ground units to appreciate the capabilities and limitations of their supporting arm. A perfect meeting of minds must exist. Only through continued training with one another, constantly observing each other's tactics, and actual sympathy for each other's problems may such coordination be achieved.

Marine pilots are trained for the support of landing operations in all its phases, from covering a convoy during its approach to the target to giving close-in support to Fleet Marine Force ground units engaged on the beach; it is in this latter phase that Marine air has become especially proficient. Pilots supporting Marines on the ground must be acquainted with Fleet Marine Force tactics, dispositions, and formations, must recognize Marine uniforms, equipment, and installations, and must be conversant with Marine lingo. Only close and continual association will attain this optimum.

An infantry officer, requesting air support, expects action immediately, *not next week*; he expects the target, *not his command post*, to be destroyed. He has neither the time nor the patience to brief his air support on factors it should already know. If the air unit has trained with the supported unit during periods of nominal peace, it will then need to know only the location and nature of its target. Other details will be worked out automatically by staffs of the respective air and ground unit commanders. Air-ground liaison, to include signals, directional markers, front-line panels, and the like, will have been perfected beforehand.

Marine Corps Aviation can neutralize targets immediately confronting front line troops. It has done it in the past as attested by the recent war; it can do it at the present time as attested by recent maneuvers; and it will do it in the future, if allowed to work along with and train with Marine infantry.

The Marine on the ground, interested in his own personal safety, to say nothing of the security of his nation, will insist on close-in air support by Marines for Marines. The Marine ground commander must have control of his air support if adequate protection is to be afforded his troops, and if his objectives are to be taken with a minimum of casualties. He cannot afford misunderstandings which may arise as a result of inter-Service differences; he must have close-in support exactly where he wants it and when he wants it. Unless he has Marines to support him, this ideal will in all likelihood be unobtainable.

If another war comes we must be completely prepared. Infantrymen who will be engaged in mortal combat desire the highly trained specialists of Marine Corps Aviation in the planes flying about overhead, prepared at any instant to render close-in air support.

With degrees from Franklin and Marshall College, Pennsylvania State College, and the University of Pennsylvania, **Major Rentz** was commissioned in the Marine Corps Reserve on January 30, 1942. Following his war service, he is presently attached to the Marine Corps Historical Division, U.S. Marine Corps Headquarters, Washington, D.C. He is the author of the Marine Corps monograph *Bougainville and the Northern Solomons*.

5   "Right on the Button: Marine Close Air Support in Korea"

Admiral John S. Thach, USN (Ret.)

U.S. Naval Institute *Proceedings*
(November 1975): 54–56

Less than five years after World War II ended, the Navy–Marine Corps team was again in combat—this time in Korea. One of the Navy's top fighter pilots of the earlier conflict, Captain John S. Thach, was commanding officer of the escort carrier Sicily *(CVE-118). As an unofficial "Marine carrier," her entire "air wing" consisted of 24 F4U Corsairs of VMF-214, the "Black Sheep" squadron made famous in World War II by Medal of Honor winner Gregory "Pappy" Boyington. The following account is based on recollections that Admiral Thach recorded as part of the Naval Institute's Oral History Program.*

THE U.S. AIR FORCE wasn't too interested in close air support. The people in high command in the Air Force were primarily hepped on the big-bomber idea—that you didn't even need troops to win a war. Just fly over and bomb them, and then wait for a telegram saying that they surrender. So they were utterly unprepared to do close air support the way it had to be done if you were going to help the troops at the front lines.

And it wasn't a matter of just curing a communications problem. It was a matter of education over a long period and experience and doctrine built up.

The Army must have been giving the Air Force hell at that time, because the Air Force even started repeating their screams to the fast carriers, "Please come, we need this, and we need it urgently, and we think it's the most important of anything you're doing," and so forth. I listened on the close air support radio many times.

By this time there really wasn't any Fifth Air Force, Korea. The Fifth Air Force was back in Japan. On one occasion, the Air Force F-80s came over from Fukuoka, Japan, and the front line was just near the end of their range. They'd call the controller and say, "Give me a target. Give me a target. I've only got five minutes more. Got to go back." When the controller asked the pilot for his ordnance load, he responded, "I've got two 100-pound bombs. Hurry up."

I heard that many times, and finally I heard someone—I think it was an Air Force controller—say, "Well, take your two little firecrackers and drop them up the road somewhere because I've got something [a carrier plane] coming in that has a load."

On 2 August 1950, a little more than a month after the war began, the *Sicily* arrived in Kobe, Japan. I'd just got the brow over when a call came up, "Captain, Tokyo wants you on the telephone." It was the duty officer at ComNavFE (Commander Naval Forces Far East) asking, "How soon can you get under way?"

"Well," I said, "there's a lot of spares and stuff here to be put aboard. I think I could get under way first thing in the morning."

He said, "You don't understand. I mean how soon can you get under way right now?" And he said this over the phone in plain English and added, "Because if you don't, there won't be any use in getting under way. It'll be too late."

We loaded as much as we could in half an hour, then left for Korea. On 3 August, we landed the Marine squadron aboard and flew our first flight in close air support. My orders from ComNavFE gave me complete freedom to go in where I could help anybody I wanted to. So that's what we did. Flying some close air support strikes that day, we started up the west coast of Korea. I had an idea of going to see what was on the roads in the Inchon-Seoul area. As it turned out, they wanted me up there anyway. We found quite a few trucks on the road and one pilot: Major Kenneth L. Reusser, executive officer of VMF-214. We later gave him the name of "Rice-Paddy Reusser" because he was forever getting shot down and ending up in a rice paddy. You know how they fertilize those rice paddies out there, and we told him if he didn't find a better-smelling place to land, we weren't going to let him aboard the next time he had a forced landing!

He was giving it the usual very-low-altitude look that professionals in close air support always do. He was flying down below treetop level, and he was shot at by some antiaircraft fire, and he thought, "Well, now what are they trying to protect?" This was between Inchon and Seoul. He went back and saw a large barnlike structure, so he flew down and looked into the window and saw a lot of vehicles in there, a tank close against the wall, and what appeared to be other tanks in the building. It may have been a tank-repair place.

He didn't have much ammunition left—a couple of rockets—so he thought, "I won't attack it now. I'll go back and come back with a big load." He came back aboard and said, "There's a big jackpot there, and I want to lead the very next strike back." He went back with plenty of bombs, rockets, and napalm and just destroyed the whole thing, ruined it. You could never find such a target while flying at high altitude. They were pretty good at camouflage, anyway, and this was the son of thing it took.

On board the *Sicily,* I made a practice of talking with every pilot after he came back. I didn't have them come up to the bridge where most captains stay all the time they're under way. I went down to the ready room where their own intelligence officer interrogated them after every strike. I missed hardly any of the debriefings from mikes because they had all the charts and everything that they could refer to down there and didn't have to bring all that paraphernalia up on the bridge. Besides giving me information I needed, I think it was good for the pilots too. We got to know each other pretty well, and it got to the point where they would make little jokes, and so would I. It was a very healthy, wonderful situation. I had a tremendous admiration for those people, and it grew and grew.

These Marine pilots of VMF-214 were all quite experienced. They weren't young kids. Most of them were married and had children, and they took their work seriously. They really were the top pros in the business, I think, in the whole world. They were heavily decorated from World War II. They knew the business of close air support. Every one of those pilots had had infantry training, and so the ground-air team of the Marine was really proficient.

On 7 August, the First Provisional Marine Brigade, which had landed at Pusan and gotten into position under Brigadier General Edward A. Craig, attacked westward from Masan toward Chinju. This was the first time the whole organization of the escort carriers (the *Sicily* and the USS *Badoeng Strait* [CVE-116]) with the Corsairs and the Marine ground forces got into action with everything there for coordination.

It was a beautiful thing to listen to. I couldn't *see* it, but I knew what was going on. It was just like going from confusing darkness into bright daylight. The coordination was just perfect, and everything clicked just the way it should. When the pilots came back, they would give a big sigh of relief and say, "Now we're doing what we're supposed to do in the right way."

One of the times we sent some planes over to support the First Marine Brigade, the Army had a patrol that really wanted help and was willing to work for it. They were so enthused about the *Sicily* Corsairs that before releasing the plane after he'd expended his ammunition in helping to break up enemy concentrations, they'd beg him to come back the next day. The words were sometimes, "Please, please, come back tomorrow. We'll take that airfield back again. If you'll just come back tomorrow, we can do it together." It would almost bring tears to your eyes to realize how much these Army troops over there wanted some real good close air support. They hadn't ever had it before. One of them said, "We had close air support like I've never heard of before. This is something I didn't realize could happen."

The Marine forward air controller on the ground was often an aviator. He and the ground troops knew each other's business because they trained at it. They would sometimes be out in front of the front lines. Sometimes they'd be in a little jeep or tank or just crawling along and dragging the communications equipment in the bushes.

One time, the controller said, "I want just one plane of the four to come down and make a dummy run. Don't drop anything. I'm going to coach you onto a big gun, a piece of artillery that's giving us a lot of trouble. I'm very close to it, but I can't do anything about it. It's just over a little knoll." He described the terrain and described everything, just as it was and so forth. So the leader came down in his Corsair, and he was coached all the way down, the air controller practically flying the airplane for him. Then he said, "Now, do you see it?"

And he said, "Yes, I see it."

"OK, then, go on back up and come down and put a 5ao-pound bomb on it. But be very careful."

So he came down and released his bomb, hit it, and it exploded.

The controller said, "Right on the button. That's all, don't need you any more."

The pilot answered, "Just a minute. While I was on the way down, on the right-hand side of my gun sight, I saw a big tank. I couldn't see it all. It was under a bush, but how about that target?"

And the controller said, "I told you I was close. Let it alone; that tank is me."

"Marine Aviation in Vietnam, 1962–1970"

6

Lieutenant General Keith B. McCutcheon, USMC

U.S. Naval Institute *Proceedings* (May 1971): 122–55

The Beginning

Marine Corps aviation involvement in Vietnam began on Palm Sunday 1962, when a squadron of UH-34 helicopters landed at Soc Trang in the Delta. The squadron was Marine Medium Helicopter Squadron 362 (HMM-362), commanded by Lieutenant Colonel Archie J. Clapp.

Three U.S. Army helicopter companies were already in Vietnam, and the Secretary of Defense had approved deployment of one more unit to Vietnam. The Marine Corps seized this opportunity to fly toward the sound of the drums and offered to send a squadron. They recommended Da Nang as the area of operations, since it was that area to which Marines were committed in various contingency plans. The Commander, United States Military Assistance Command, Vietnam (ComUSMACV), decreed, however, that the need at the moment was in the Delta since that Vietnamese Army corps area was the only one of the four corps areas in Vietnam that did not have any helicopter support.

Colonel John F. Carey was the commanding officer of the Marine task unit of which HMM-362 was a part. He arrived at Soc Trang on 9 April, and over the ensuing five days an element of Marine Air Base

Squadron 16 (MABS-16) arrived aboard Marine KC-130 aircraft from the Marine Corps Air Facility at Futema, Okinawa. Squadron HMM-362, augmented by three O-1 observation aircraft, embarked in the USS *Princeton* (LPH-5) at Okinawa and arrived off the Mekong Delta at dawn on Palm Sunday, 15 April. The squadron's helicopters completed unloading the unit's equipment and were ashore by late afternoon. The Marine task unit which was to be known as "Shufly" was established ashore.

The mission of this unit was to provide helicopter troop and cargo lift for Vietnamese Army units and its first operation was one week later, on Easter Sunday. The squadron continued to operate until August when it was relieved by HMM-163, commanded by Lieutenant Colonel Robert L. Rathbun.

In September 1962, the Marines were ordered by ComUSMACV to move to Da Nang, the high threat area, an area with which Marine planners had become well acquainted in contingency plans, war games, and advanced base problems. Some had been there before. In April 1954, Lieutenant Colonel Julius W. Ireland had landed at Da Nang airfield with Marine Attack Squadron 324 (VMA-324) and turned over twenty-five A-1 propeller driven dive bombers to the hard-pressed French. Now he was back as a colonel. He had replaced Colonel Carey as the commander of "Shufly."

The Marines initially occupied two areas on the air base. The helicopter maintenance and parking area was southeast of the runway. The billeting area was across the base on the western side, about two miles away. In those days there was not much traffic at Da Nang, so the Marines got into the habit of driving across the runway as the shortest route to commute back and forth. Four years later, this would be one of the two or three busiest airfields in the world.

In late 1964, the runway was extended to 10,000 feet, and a perimeter road, half surfaced and half dirt, was built around the base.

The Land and the Weather

Da Nang is the second largest city in Vietnam and the largest in the Vietnamese Army's I Corps Tactical Zone, commonly called I Corps and abbreviated as ICTZ. By 1970 Da Nang would have a population of approximately 400,000. An exact count is impossible because of the influx of war victims and refugees. ICTZ consists of the northernmost five provinces of Vietnam: Quang Tri, Thua Thien, Quang Nam, Quang Tin, and Quang Ngai. The length of ICTZ is about 225 miles, and its width varies from 40 to 75 miles. Da Nang is approximately in the center of the north-south dimension and is on the coast. Hue, the next largest city, with a population of about 200,000, is roughly halfway between the Demilitarized Zone (DMZ) and Da Nang. Hue, the old capital of Annam, is inland a few miles on the Perfume River. About halfway between Da Nang and the southern boundary of I Corps is a sandy area on the littoral of the South China Sea that came to be known as Chu Lai.

Called Tourane by the French, Da Nang sits on a fairly large bay which provides a roomy, if not particularly safe, deep water harbor and anchorage, although in 1965 it had few facilities to unload ships in any numbers. To the north of the bay are the Hai Van Mountains, called "Col des Nuages" by the French, which stretch eastward from the Annamite Mountain chain to the sea. These mountains are an important factor in I Corps weather and, in fact, form a barrier which can cause one side to be under instrument Bight rule conditions and the other side under visual Bight rule conditions.

East of Da Nang, across the Song Han River, is the Tien Sha Peninsula that juts past the city to provide a large breakwater for the bay. At the end of the peninsula is a massive 2,000-foot hill known as Monkey Mountain.

The terrain in I Corps rises as you move inland from the Coast. In general, there are three broad regions: the coastal lowlands where rice paddies abound, and there 85 per cent of the three million people live;

the piedmont area of slightly higher ground which permits cultivation of other crops, and which is home for most of the remainder of the people; and the hill country, or Annamite chain. These mountains go up to 5,000 feet and higher, some rather precipitously. For the most part they are heavily forested and in places there is a triple canopy which makes observation of the ground impossible.

Running generally from west to east, from the high ground to the sea, is a series of rivers and streams which follow the valleys and natural drainage routes. They are generally unnavigable except for small, oar-propelled, shallow draft boats, but they do offer routes from Laos to the provinces.

The northeast monsoon begins in October and ends in March. September and April are more or less transition months. Rainfall increases in September and October, and by November the northeast monsoon is well established over ICTZ. Weak cold fronts periodically move southward and usually there is an increase in the intensity of low level winds (rising sometimes 20 to 50 knots). This is called a "surge." The "surge" causes ceilings of 1,000 to 1,500 feet with rain, drizzle, and fog restricting visibility to one or two miles. Occasionally the ceiling drops to 200 feet and the visibility to half a mile. After the initial "surge" has passed, the winds begin to decrease and the weather will stabilize with ceilings of 1,500 to 2,000 feet prevailing. Visibility will fluctuate from seven miles or more to three miles or less owing to intermittent periods of fog or precipitation. Cloud tops are seldom above 10,000 feet.

The kind of weather just described was called "crachin" by the French. It can prevail for a few days at a time early in the monsoon season or for several weeks during the high intensity months. As winds decrease, the weather generally improves. When the lower level winds decrease to less than ten knots, or if the wind shifts from the northeast to a northwest or a southerly direction, a break in the weather is usually experienced. Such a break will result in scattered to broken clouds with bases at 2,000 to 3,000 feet and unrestricted visibility and may persist for a week before another "surge" develops.

During December, the monsoon strengthens, and in January, when the Siberian high pressure cell reaches its maximum intensity, the northeast monsoon also develops to its greatest extent. Little change can be expected over ICTZ in February, although "surges" are generally weaker and more shallow than in January. By mid-March the flow pattern is poorly defined and the monsoon becomes weak. During April, traces of the southwest monsoon begin to appear and there is a noticeable decrease in cloudiness over the area. From then through August, the weather in ICTZ is hot and humid, with little rainfall.

The northeast monsoon had a direct impact on all military operations in ICTZ and especially on air operations. Because they can operate with lower ceilings and visibility minimums than fixed-wing aircraft, the helicopters would often perform their missions when the fixed-wing could not, at least along the flat coastal region. Inland, however, the hills and mountains made even helicopter flying hazardous at best. The pilots all developed a healthy respect for the northeast monsoon.

Early Days at Da Nang

HMM-163 was relieved by HMM-162 in January 1963. Over the next two years other HMMs followed: 261, 361, 364, 162 for a second time, 365, and, finally, 163 for its second tour. Half the Corps' UH-34 squadrons had received invaluable combat experience before the commitment of the Marine Corps air-ground team of division-wing size.

In April 1963, an infantry platoon from the 3d Marine Division (3dMarDiv) was airlifted from Okinawa to join "Shufly." Its mission was to provide increased security for the base. In a modest way, the air-ground team was in being in Vietnam.

Brigadier General Raymond G. Davis, Commanding General of the 9th Marine Expeditionary Brigade (9thMEB), flew to Da Nang in August

1964, shortly after the Tonkin Gulf affair, and completed plans to reinforce the Marines based there in the event of an emergency. He then joined his command afloat with the Amphibious Ready Group of the Seventh Fleet. This Group was to be on and off various alert conditions for some months to come.

Early in December 1964, "Shufly" received a new title by direction of Lieutenant General Victor H. Krulak, Commanding General of the Fleet Marine Force, Pacific (FMFPac). It was now called Marine Unit Vietnam, or MUV for short.

Another aviation unit began arriving at Da Nang on 8 February 1965. This was the 1st Light Anti-Aircraft Missile (LAAM) Battalion, commanded by Lieutenant Colonel Bertram E. Cook, Jr. The battalion was equipped with Hawk surface-to-air missiles. Battery "A," commanded by Captain Leon E. Obenhaus, arrived by air and was established on the base just to the west of the runway. Within twenty-four hours it was ready for operation. The remainder of the battalion came by ship from Okinawa, arriving at Da Nang later in the month. This battalion had been sent to Okinawa in December 1964, from its base in California, as a result of ComUSMACV's request for missiles for air defense. The decision was made to retain the unit on Okinawa instead of sending it to Vietnam, but when the Viet Cong attacked Pleiku on 7 February, the United States retaliated with an air strike in North Vietnam. An order to deploy the Hawks to Da Nang was made at the same time. As in the case of Cuba in 1962, when a crisis situation developed, Marine missile units were among the first to be deployed.

By this time MUV was pretty well established on the west side of the Da Nang air base in an old French army compound. Colonel John H. King, Jr., was in command. The helicopters were moved from their first maintenance and parking area, and were now located on the southwest corner of the field. A rather large sheet metal lean-to had been made available by the Vietnamese Air Force (VNAF) to serve as a hangar. The parking apron was blacktop and was adequate for about two squadrons of UH-34s.

Buildup

Late in February 1965, President Johnson made a decision to commit a Marine brigade to protect the air base at Da Nang from Communist attack. On 8 March the 9thMEB, including the 3d Battalion, 9th Marines, was ordered to land. They had been afloat and ready for such an operation for several months. Brigadier General Frederick C. Karch was then the commander of the brigade.

The 1st Battalion, 3d Marines, meanwhile had been alerted on Okinawa for a possible airlift. It, too, was ordered to Da Nang on 8 March. Because of the congestion which developed on the airfield, ComUSMACV ordered a temporary cessation to the lift. It was resumed on the 11th and the battalion arrived in Da Nang on the 12th.

Squadron HMM-365, commanded by Lieutenant Colonel Joseph Koler, Jr., was embarked in the *Princeton*. Koler's UH-34s were flown to the airfield at Da Nang, but the crews re-embarked in the *Princeton* for the voyage to Okinawa. Aircrews and squadron personnel of Lieutenant Colonel Oliver W. Curtis' HMM-162 were airlifted by KC-130 from Okinawa to Da Nang to take over the UH-34s left by HMM-365.

Brigadier General Karch took operational control of all Marine aviation units that were already ashore. He also established an MEB command post in the same old French compound where Colonel King was set up. Colonel King had had the foresight to contact General Thi, who commanded I Corps and the ICTZ, to get permission to use some additional buildings.

The air component of the 9thMEB now included two HMMs and one LAAM battalion. Colonel King remained in command of the air units. He also received some service support elements from Marine Aircraft Group 16 (MAG-16) based at Futema, Okinawa, and since his command was now integrated into the MEB, the MUV was deactivated and MAG-16(–) took its place. A rear echelon of MAG-16 remained at Futema, Okinawa.

Requests for additional military forces were submitted by ComUSMACV. One 15-plane Marine Fighter/Attack Squadron (VMFA) was authorized to deploy to Da Nang. VMFA-531 based at Atsugi, Japan, and commanded by Lieutenant Colonel William C. McGraw, Jr., received the order on 10 April. By dusk on the 11th, the aircraft and most of the men were in Da Nang, having flown there directly, refueling in the air from Marine KC-130 tankers as they went. On 13 April, McGraw led twelve of his F-4Bs on their first combat mission in South Vietnam, in support of U.S. Marine ground troops. The F-4 was an aircraft that would perform either air-to-air missions against hostile aircraft or air-to-ground strikes in support of friendly troops.

As the tempo of retaliatory strikes against North Vietnam by the Navy and Air Force increased, the enemy air defense began to include greater numbers of radar-controlled weapon systems. The sole source of tactical electronic warfare aircraft readily available to counter the new enemy defense was Marine Composite Reconnaissance Squadron One (VMCJ-1) at Iwakuni, Japan. On 10 April 1965, the Commander-in-Chief, Pacific (CinCPac), ordered the deployment of an EF-10B detachment to Vietnam. The detachment, led by Lieutenant Colonel Otis W. Corman, arrived in Da Nang the same day. The electronic warfare aircraft (EF-10Bs and later EA-6As) began to provide support to Marine, Navy, and Air Force strike aircraft. The photo-reconnaissance aircraft (RF-8s and RF-4s) arrived later and performed primarily in support of Marine units, but they also supported Army units in I Corps and flew bomb damage assessment missions north of the DMZ.

Southeast Asia was an area familiar to the pilots of VMCJ-1. Detachments of RF-8As, the photographic aircraft of the squadron, had been aboard various carriers in the Gulf of Tonkin continually since May 1964, when CinCPac initiated the Yankee Team operations to conduct photo reconnaissance over Laos. Detachment pilots were also on hand to participate in the Navy's first air strikes against North Vietnam, and they continued photographic reconnaissance activities as part of carrier air wings until the detachment rejoined the parent unit at Da Nang in December 1965.

Colonel King now had an air group that contained elements of two jet squadrons, two helicopter squadrons, a Hawk missile battalion, and air control facilities so he could operate a Direct Air Support Center (DASC) and an Air Support Radar Team (ASRT). He also had the support of a detachment of KC-130 transports that were based in Japan.

The month of May was one of further growth and change. Several additional infantry battalions arrived and elements of MAG-12 landed at Chu Lai to the south of Da Nang. Major General William R. Collins, Commanding General, 3dMarDiv, arrived on 3 May from Okinawa. He set up an advance division command post, and on 6 May he established the Third Marine Expeditionary Force (III MEF); the 9thMEB was deactivated. Within a few days the title of III MEF was changed to Third Marine Amphibious Force (III MAF). The term "expeditionary" seemed to conjure up unhappy memories of the earlier ill-fated French expeditionary corps. And some believed "amphibious" was more appropriate for a Marine command in any event.

On 11 May, Major General Paul J. Fontana opened an advance command post of the 1st Marine Aircraft Wing (1stMAW) in the same compound. On 24 May, Brigadier General Keith B. McCutcheon, assistant wing commander, arrived to relieve General Fontana in the advance command post, and on 5 June he relieved him as Commanding General of the 1stMAW. The day before, Major General Lewis W. Walt relieved Collins as Commanding General, 3dMarDiv and III MAF. McCutcheon became Deputy Commander, III MAF, and Tactical Air Commander.

The Marine Air-Ground Team was in place. The 1stMAW now had elements of a headquarters group and two aircraft groups in Vietnam. Additional units were waiting to deploy and still others were requested. It was but the beginning of a steady Marine buildup in I Corps. It was summer and the weather was hot and dry. The heavy rains were not due to start until September.

Resources

Bases

The major constraint to receiving any more air units was the lack of adequate bases.

Da Nang Air Base was one of only three jet-capable airfields in all of Vietnam, and the only one in I Corps; the others were Bien Hoa and Tan Son Nhut, both near Saigon. In 1965, Da Nang had one 10,000-foot paved runway with a parallel taxiway. Less than half the length of the runway on the eastern side of the field had associated ramp space for parking aircraft. On the western side there was a blacktop parking apron that could accommodate about two squadrons of helicopters.

A military construction board was formed in III MAF and a list of requirements was prepared and submitted to higher authority. A second runway and taxiway had already been approved at the end of March for Da Nang as well as adequate hardstand and maintenance areas on the western side of the field. This would eventually accommodate one Marine Aircraft Group, a Support Group, and a Navy unit (Fleet Air Support Unit, Da Nang) which arrived in April 1968, in order to carry out various functions for the Seventh Fleet. The eastern side of the field would then be released to the U.S. Air Force and the Vietnamese Air Force. Before this construction could be undertaken, however, a base had to be made available for the helicopters then at Da Nang. And still another base was required for a second jet group.

There were several restrictions confronting III MAF as far as construction was concerned. First, was the problem of obtaining real estate. This was a laborious and time consuming administrative process. Second, was the need to relocate the Vietnamese families living on the desired site. Equally important to the Vietnamese was the relocation of their ancestral grave sites. Third, there was inadequate engineering help available in Vietnam to build everything required, so priorities had to be established. And finally, security forces had to be provided, and any unit assigned to this task meant fewer troops for other tactical operations.

SATS and Chu Lai

A second jet base was essential. Through the foresight of Lieutenant General Krulak, a likely site had been picked out about fifty miles south of Da Nang for a Short Airfield for Tactical Support (SATS). General Krulak had recommended it almost a year before to Admiral Sharp, who was CinCPac. Admiral Sharp and General Westmoreland had been discussing the need for another jet base somewhere in South Vietnam. General Krulak's main concern was to have a jet airfield in I Corps, where his Marines were to be committed if the contingency plans were implemented. Finally, on 30 March 1965, Secretary McNamara approved installation of a SATS at Chu Lai. Chu Lai was not a recognized name on Vietnamese maps at that time and the rumor is that Krulak gave it that name when he chose the place. Chu Lai reportedly is part of his name in Chinese.

By virtue of their experience in Naval Aviation, Marine aviators had long recognized the advantage of being able to approximate a carrier deck sort of operation on the beach. They realized that many areas of the world did not have adequate airfields, and that normal construction methods took too long. Something that approached an "instant airfield" was required.

In the mid-fifties, the Marine Corps Development Center at Quantico, Virginia, intensified development of both the concept and the hardware to realize this project. They visualized a 2,000-foot airstrip that could handle a Marine Aircraft Group of two or three aircraft squadrons. The essential components of such a base would include a suitable surface for the runway, taxiways, and hardstands; a means of arresting the aircraft on landing similar to that on a carrier deck; a catapult or other means to assist in launching the aircraft; provisions for refueling, rearming, and maintenance; air control facilities; and, of course, all the necessities for housekeeping. The installation time was to be from 72 to 96 hours.

Various projects were already underway that could provide solutions to some of these problems. Others had to be started. Furthermore, the entire concept had to be pulled together into a single system. Naturally, a name for the system was required and a name was found—SATS—Short Airfield for Tactical Support.

The kind of surface material to use was one of the harder problems to solve. Fabrics, plastics, soil stabilizers, and many other ideas were tried, but none was able to cope with the impact and static loads of aircraft operations and the temperature of jet exhaust. Finally, attention was directed to metals, and eventually a solid aluminum plank was developed which promised to do the job. It was known as AM-2. A single piece of this mat measures two feet by 12 feet and weighs 140 pounds. The individual pieces are capable of being interconnected and locked in place, thus providing a smooth, flat surface that is both strong and durable.

The arrested landing problem was already in hand with the use of modified shipboard arresting gear. Development of improved equipment was initiated, nevertheless, and the M-21 was the result. This is a dry friction, energy-absorbing device using a tape drive with a wire pendant stretching across the runway. This arresting gear is now standard in the Corps.

Launching in a short space was a bigger problem. JATO (Jet Assisted Take-Off) bottles were available, but these could be a logistical burden over a long period of time. A catapult was desired. Development and testing were not complete in early 1965, but progress was promising.

The refueling problem was solved by adapting the Amphibious Assault Bulk Fuel Handling System (AABFHS) to the airfield environment. The result was the Tactical Airfield Fuel Dispensing System, or TAFDS. This system used the same 10,000-gallon collapsible tanks, hoses, pumps, and water separators as the AABFHS, but it added special nozzles for refueling aircraft: they were single-point refueling nozzles for jets, and filling station gooseneck types for helos and light aircraft.

In a similar manner, all of the other requirements were analyzed and action was taken to find a solution. By May 1965, all were available except the catapult, but JATO was on hand, and Marine A-4s were modified to use it.

The concept of SATS visualized seizing an old World War II airstrip or some similar and reasonably flat surface that required a minimum amount of earth moving, and installing a 2,000-foot SATS thereon in about 72 to 96 hours. This would permit flight operations to commence, while improvements and expansion could be conducted simultaneously.

Chu Lai did not meet all the requirements visualized by SATS planners. It was not a World War II abandoned airfield. The soil wasn't even dirt. It was sand. And there was lots of it.

But Chu Lai was on the sea, it had a semi-protected body of water behind a peninsula that could be developed into an LST port, it could be defended, and there were few hamlets in the area that would have to be relocated. All things considered, Chu Lai was the most likely site on which to build a new air base.

On 7 May 1965, Naval Mobile Construction Battalion 10 (NMCB-10), under Commander J. M. Bannister, crossed the deep sandy beach at Chu Lai along with the 4th Marine Regiment and elements of MAG-12. The Seabees went to work on 9 May, constructing the first SATS ever installed in a combat environment.

The landing force commander at Chu Lai was Brigadier General Marion E. Carl, one of the Corps' most famous aviators. He had brought his 1st Marine Brigade from Hawaii to the Western Pacific in March and although that Brigade was disbanded, Carl had become Commanding General of the 3dMEB. As there were no stakes to mark the previously chosen site, he had a hand in picking the exact spot where the runway should go.

The sand proved to be a formidable enemy. Unloading from the ships was hampered, as driving vehicles through the sand was most difficult. Tracked vehicles were essential to move the rubber-tired ones. It required a superhuman effort to get the job done.

The general construction scheme was to excavate some locally available soil, called laterite, and use it as a sub-base between the sand and aluminum matting. Before that could be done, a road had to be built from the site of the airfield to the laterite deposit. This was done, but the combination of temperatures around the hundred mark and the effect of sand on automotive and engineering equipment slowed the progress of construction. Both men and mechanical equipment grew tired quickly in this hostile environment. Needless to say, no one expected to finish in four days. Even thirty looked totally unrealistic, but that was the goal. In spite of the problems and obstacles, Lieutenant General Krulak bet Major General Richard G. Stilwell, Chief of Staff of MACV, that a squadron would be operating there within 30 days.

By Memorial Day, approximately four thousand feet of mat and several hundred feet of taxiway were in place. Chu Lai was ready to receive aircraft, but tropical storms prevented the planes from flying from the Philippines to Vietnam until 1 June. Shortly after 0800 on that date, Colonel John D. Noble, Commanding Officer of MAG-12, landed an A-4 into the mobile arresting gear on the aluminum runway. He was followed by three others, and, later in the day, four more arrived. About 1300, the first combat mission was launched using JATO with Lieutenant Colonel Robert W. Baker, Commanding Officer of VMA-225, leading.

General Krulak paid off his bet of a case of Scotch to Stilwell on the basis that a full squadron was not operating there in the forecast time, only half of one.

But construction continued and, as additional taxiway was built, more planes came in. Meanwhile operations continued on a daily basis.

The laterite, however, simply wasn't doing the job, so when 8,000 feet of runway was installed, it was decided to operate from the southern 4,000 feet and to re-lay the northern 4,000 feet, which were the first to go down. As it turned out, after the northern half was redone, the other half had to have the same treatment, and then the cycle was repeated still another time when, at last, the right sub-base combination was found.

Various techniques were tried, including watering and packing the sand down without any other material, shooting the sand with a light layer of asphalt, and finally a combination of the latter and using a thin plastic membrane under the matting to keep rain from settling into the soil and undermining the runway surface.

Drainage was essential, of course, as any standing water under the mat set up a pumping action as aircraft rolled over the mat, which was particularly noticeable when a transport like a KC-130 landed and rolled out.

During these periods of 4,000-foot operations, JATO was used when high temperatures and heavy bomb loads required it. In addition, a Marine KC-130 tanker was kept available to top off A-4s after take-off, by in-flight refueling.

A catapult was installed in April 1966, so all SATS components were then in place. The catapult was tested and evaluated under combat conditions but was not actually required on that date because of the length of the runway. It was used, but not on a sustained basis.

The SATS concept was proven under combat conditions at Chu Lai. The AM-2 mat became a hot item, and production of it was increased markedly in the United States, as all Services sought it. It was used for non-SATS airfields and helicopter pads, and became as commonplace in Southeast Asia as was the pierced steel plank (PSP) in the Southwest Pacific in World War II. Likewise, TAFDS components became a common sight, and their flexible fuel lines could be seen almost anywhere.

The original "tinfoil strip," as it came to be called, was still in operation late in 1970, more than five years after it was laid down. Not even the planners back in Quantico in 1955 ever envisioned that someone would install a short airfield for tactical support on sand and leave it there for five years. But this is exactly what was done at Chu Lai.

Ky Ha and Marble Mountain
The small civilian airfield at Phu Bai, South of Hue, could accommodate one helicopter squadron, which was required in that area to support

an infantry battalion that was assigned to secure the region in 1965. But in addition, two major helo bases were required in relatively short order: first, to take care of MAG-36, which had been alerted to deploy from Santa Ana, California; and second, to free Da Nang of its rotary wing aircraft, so that construction of the parallel runway there could be started.

The peninsula to the northeast of Chu Lai provided a likely site for a helo group as well as an air control squadron. The Seabees began preparation of a flat area and laid down several kinds of metal matting, but they had no time to do anything else in the way of preparing for MAG-36's arrival. The group departed from the West Coast in August 1965, and arrived off Chu Lai early in September. They unloaded, moved ashore, and set about building their own camp. At night they also established their own perimeter defense as there was no infantry to do it for them. And, almost as soon as they landed, the rains began. Whereas at Chu Lai it was sand, at Ky Ha it was pure, unadulterated mud. The base was named Ky Ha after the village nearest the site.

For MAG-16, a site had been chosen east of Da Nang just north of Marble Mountain. There was a beautiful stretch of sandy beach along the South China Sea and just inland was a fine expanse of land covered with coniferous trees ten to twenty feet high. Unfortunately, as soon as word got out that Marines were going to construct an air base there, the local Vietnamese came onto the land in droves and removed all the trees including the roots, instead of the few that had to be removed to build the runway and parking areas. Thus, the troops and other inhabitants lost the protection these trees would have afforded against sun, wind, and erosion.

The civilian construction combine in Vietnam, Raymond, Morrison, Knudson-Brown, Root, and Jones (RMK-BRJ), received the job of building the helicopter facility at Marble Mountain. It was sufficiently advanced by late August 1965 to allow MAG-16 to move from Da Nang and operate at the new facility.

All during the summer, the question of whether or not another SATS type airfield should be constructed in ICTZ was under serious consideration. There were four likely sites: from north to south, Phu Bai, Marble Mountain Air Facility, Tam Ky, and Quang Ngai. After much study and many messages, the idea was abandoned when it became clear that Da Nang plus Chu Lai would be adequate.

On the night of 27 October 1965, the enemy executed a coordinated sapper attack against Da Nang, Marble Mountain, and Chu Lai. The attack on Da Nang was thwarted by artillery fire against one column to the west, and by an alert ambush against a second force to the south.

At midnight, three sapper teams hit Marble Mountain Air Facility. The team from the north was met by aviation specialists standing guard duty and every attacker was killed. The southern team was driven off. But the one from the west managed to get on to the parking area and several of the enemy raced from helo to helo throwing charges into each. In short order, the place was a mass of burning aircraft. Over twenty were damaged beyond repair, and an equal number required varying degrees of repair.

At Chu Lai only a handful of sappers made it to the flight line, and half of them were killed. A few A-4s were damaged, two beyond repair.

Air bases were to become prime targets. They required close-in defense in depth to make sapper infiltration unprofitable, and they required an outer mobile defense by infantry to ward off rockets and mortars. The ground units did a superb job in keeping the enemy off balance, so that only a few rockets and mortars found profitable targets. Further, aviation and ground personnel tightened their perimeter defense, so never again was there an infiltration which equaled the success of the October attack.

Da Nang

Once MAG-16 had vacated the west side of Da Nang, construction could begin on the parallel runway and taxiway. Plans were made to construct the northern and southern concrete touchdown pads and connecting taxiways to the east runway first, the MAG operating and maintenance area on the northwest corner of the base second, the remainder of the runway third, and the parallel taxiway last. The two touchdown pads were required first because there was an urgent requirement to move VMCJ-1 from the parking apron on the east side of the field. Furthermore, an F-8 squadron was authorized for Da Nang, but there was no ramp space. The northern touchdown pad would provide ramp space for these two jet squadrons. The southern pad would provide a place to operate the KC-130s and C-117s.

The 1stMAW did not desire to have the entire runway completed before the MAG operating area was, because if it had been, it would have been used as a runway and not for ramp space. This priority was given to the completion of jobs because the engineer work-force was not adequate to undertake them all simultaneously. Although another runway was sorely needed, parking space was the more urgent requirement. Why wasn't a SATS built so a runway would be available at the same time parking space was? Because what was needed was a long runway for the long haul that would accommodate Marine, Navy, Air Force, commercial, and miscellaneous aircraft of all sizes.

MAG-11 moved into Da Nang from its base at Atsugi, Japan, in July 1965, and took command of the jet squadrons which up to that time had been under control of MAG-16. Colonel Robert F. Conley commanded MAG-11. The F-8 squadron, Marine All-Weather Fighter Squadron 312 (VMF[AW]-312), commanded by Lieutenant Colonel Richard B. Newport, arrived at Da Nang in December 1965 and occupied the completed northern touchdown pad along with VMCJ-1, which had moved over from the east side of the base.

The MAG operating area for MAG-11 and the west runway were completed late in 1966, and the last Marine flight operations were then moved from the east side of the base to the west side.

Chu Lai West

A 10,000-foot conventional concrete runway and associated taxiways, high speed turnoffs, and ramp space for two MAGs was begun at Chu Lai, to the west of the SATS strip, early in 1966 and completed that October. Marine Air Group 13 arrived from Iwakuni, Japan, and occupied the new base. This Air Group had been stationed at Kaneohe, Hawaii, as part of the 1st Marine Brigade. It deployed to the Western Pacific with the Brigade and Brigadier General Carl in March, but bided its time in Okinawa and later in Japan, until a base was available for it in Vietnam. Beginning in the fall of 1967, both MAGs 12 and 13 operated from the concrete runway, and the SATS strip was made available to the Army for helos and light aircraft.

An AM-2 runway, complete with catapult and arresting gear, was constructed to connect the northern ends of the concrete and "tinfoil" runways. This provided for a cross-wind runway, about 4,800 feet in length, as well as an interconnection of the two fields for aircraft movement on the ground.

Helo Bases in Northern ICTZ

As the center of gravity of Marine operations moved north, the helos followed. Late in 1967, Phu Bai was expanded to accommodate a full helicopter group, and MAG-36 moved there from Ky Ha, which was taken over by the American Division. Later a base was established at Dong Ha to support the 3dMarDiv's operations below the DMZ. This proved to be a particularly hot area, as it came under fire with some regularity from enemy artillery north of the DMZ. In October 1967, the Quang Tri helicopter base, nine nautical miles south of Dong Ha and beyond the range of enemy artillery firing from the DMZ, was completed in a record 24 days. The helicopters were sent there from Dong Ha and operations were begun immediately. In April 1968, a provisional air group, MAG-39, was established out of 1stMAW resources in order to provide better command and control over the helicopter squadrons based at Quang Tri to better support the 3dMarDiv.

Monkey Mountain

Another formidable construction project was the emplacement of a Hawk missile battery on Monkey Mountain just east of Da Nang. The site selected was over two thousand feet above sea level and about one mile east of the Air Force radar site known as Panama. Naval Mobile Construction Battalion 9, led by Commander Richard Anderson, was given this task. A road had to be built first of all, and then the mountain peak had to be leveled in order to provide a sufficiently flat area to emplace the battery. On 1 September 1965, the site was sufficiently cleared to receive the equipment, and Captain Charles R. Keith's "B" Battery, 1st LAAM Battalion, was emplaced. As in the case of airfields, development of the site continued concurrently with operations. Late in 1966, a similar but less extensive construction effort was undertaken just to the east of Hai Van Pass, so that the LAAM Battery which was still on Da Nang Air Base could be moved to a better tactical location.

Other Operating Areas

In addition to these permanent bases, many outlying fields and expeditionary operating areas were established as the military requirement dictated. Airfields suitable for KC-130s and helos were built or improved at Khe Sanh, An Hoa, Landing Zone Baldy, Tam Ky, and Quang Ngai; and the 1stMAW at one time or another had detachments stationed at these installations to provide for air traffic control, refueling, rearming, and other essential tasks. ("Suitable for KC-130s" means about 3,000 feet of runway with some sort of hard surface.) The 1stMAW had the capability to move where the action was. Its expeditionary character was well suited to this kind of campaign.

Men, Units, and Aircraft

From the time it established its command post (CP) at Da Nang in June 1965 until April 1966, the 1stMAW maintained a rear echelon under its command at Iwakuni, Japan. During this period the 1stMAW had cognizance over all Marine Corps aviation units deployed to the Western Pacific. It rotated jet units between Japan and Vietnam and helo squadrons between Okinawa, the Special Landing Force (SLF) afloat in the Seventh Fleet, and Vietnam. It also reassigned men.

In Vietnam the wing had a Headquarters Group and four aircraft MAGs: MAG-11 and MAG-12, with jets at Da Nang and Chu Lai respectively; MAG-16 at Marble Mountain and Phu Bai with helos; and MAG-36 at Ky Ha with helos. A Service Group, stationed in Japan as part of the rear echelon, did not arrive in Vietnam until 1966, when facilities became available. The Headquarters Group and the Service Group were both reorganized in 1967 by Headquarters Marine Corps into three groups instead of two: a Headquarters Group, an Air Control Group, and a Support Group. This reflected a realignment of functions to provide better management of resources, based on experience gained in the recent move of the 1stMAW from Japan and Okinawa to Vietnam.

The first aircraft squadrons to arrive in Vietnam were from 1stMAW units in Japan and Okinawa. These were "rotational" squadrons. Each had been trained in the United States and deployed as a team to serve a 13-month tour together in WestPac. At the expiration of that tour, another squadron was scheduled to arrive to replace the old squadron on station.

Because all members of the squadron arrived at the same time, it meant they all had to be sent back to the United States at the same time. Likewise, all the men in squadrons that arrived in Vietnam from Hawaii and the United States, whether their units were rotational squadrons or not, would also have to be replaced at the same time.

The Corps could no longer support unit rotation on that scale, so it was forced to go to a system of replacement by individuals rather than by units, except in special cases. This problem arose because the Stateside training establishment became saturated with training individuals as individuals and had no time to devote to team or unit training, except for those units which were reforming with new aircraft. In the latter case, unit rotation was necessary. In order to preclude all of a unit being replaced in one month, the 1stMAW went through a reassignment program in late 1965 in an effort to smooth out the rotation dates of men's tours. All like squadrons, for example all HMMs, had their men interchanged to take advantage of different squadron arrival times in WestPac so that their losses through rotation would be spread over several months rather than one. Short touring a few men helped further to spread the losses. This program was called "Operation Mixmaster." It was a difficult one to administer but it accomplished its objective.

In April 1966, the aviation units in Japan and Okinawa were removed from the 1stMAW and established as a separate command reporting directly to FMFPac. The rotation of aircraft, men, and units in and out of Vietnam then became the direct responsibility of FMFPac in lieu of the 1stMAW. The principal reasons for this were that the 1stMAW was increasing in size to the point that the staff could not manage men and equipment spread all over the Western Pacific, and the units in Japan and Okinawa were under the operational control of the Seventh Fleet rather than under General Westmoreland in Vietnam, who did have the operational control of 1stMAW. So this realignment logically transferred administrative control to FMFPac.

When the war began in 1965, the Marine Corps was authorized 54 deployable aircraft squadrons in the Fleet Marine Forces: 30 jet, 3 propeller transport, 18 helicopter transport, and 3 observation.

After initial deployments to Vietnam in 1965, action was initiated on a priority basis to expand the Corps. Another Marine division, the 5th; one deployable helicopter group consisting of two medium helicopter squadrons; and two observation squadrons were authorized for the duration of the Southeast Asia conflict. The 5thMarDiv was organized, trained, and equipped, and elements of it were deployed to Vietnam. The helicopter group never did become fully organized or equipped. Only one of its helo squadrons was formed. Additionally, two fixed wing and two helicopter training groups, all non-deployable, were authorized for the permanent force structure, but they were not fully equipped until 1970.

The reasons that these aviation units were not completely organized and equipped were primarily time and money. All of the essential resources were long-lead-time items: pilots, technical men, and aircraft. All of them are expensive.

The Reserves could have provided trained personnel, but they were not called up in the case of the Marine Corps. The Reserve 4th Marine Aircraft Wing was not equipped with modern aircraft equivalent to the three regular wings, and it did not have anywhere near its allowance of helicopters, so even if the men had been left behind, it would not have been much help as far as aircraft were concerned.

Two years later the Department of Defense authorized the Marine Corps to reorganize its three permanent and two temporary observation squadrons into three observation and three light transport helicopter squadrons. The net result of these authorization was that the Marine Corps added one medium and three light transport helicopter squadrons, giving a total of 58 deployable squadrons.

The Arrival of New Aircraft

Aviation is a dynamic profession. The rate of obsolescence of equipment is high and new aircraft have to be placed in the inventory periodically in order to stay abreast of the requirements of modern war. In 1965, the Corps was entering a period that would see the majority of its aircraft replaced within four years.

The A-6A all-weather attack aircraft was coming into the FMF to replace six of twelve A-4 squadrons. (The Marine Corps could neither afford nor did it need to acquire a 100 per cent all-weather capability.) The squadrons retaining A-4s would get a newer and more capable series of A-4. Two-seat TA-4Fs would also become available to replace the old F-9 series used by airborne tactical air coordinators.

The F-4B was well along in replacing the F-8 in the 15 fighter squadrons, and in two years, it was to be replaced in part with an even more capable F-4J.

The RF-4 photo reconnaissance aircraft was programmed to replace the RF-8.

The EA-6A electronic warfare aircraft was procured to replace the EF-10B, which was a Korean War vintage airframe.

The O-1 was scheduled to give way to the OV-10A.

The UH-34 medium transport helicopter and the CH-37 heavy transport were to be replaced by the CH-46 and the CH-53, respectively, in the 18 transport helicopter squadrons.

The UH-1E was just coming into inventory to replace the H-43. In a few years, the AH-1G Cobra would fill a complete void. It would provide the Corps with its first gunship designed for the mission. It did not replace, but rather augmented the UH-1E. (The Marine Corps had no AC-47s, AC-117s, AC-119s, or AC-130s. Every C-47, 117, 119, and 130 the Corps had was required for its primary purpose and none was available for modification to a gunship role.)

Only the KC-130 tanker-transport did not have a programmed replacement.

New models were accepted all through the war. As each was received, a training base had to be built, not only for aircrews but also for technicians. In order to introduce a new model into the 1stMAW, a full squadron had to be trained and equipped or, in the case of reconnaissance aircraft, a detachment equivalent to one-third or one-half a squadron. As a new unit arrived in Vietnam, a similar unit with older aircraft would return to the United States to undergo reforming with new aircraft. After several like squadrons had arrived in Vietnam, they would undergo a "mixmaster" process in order to spread the rotation tour dates of the men for the same reason as the first squadrons that entered the country.

In June 1965, nine of the fixed wing and five helicopter/observation squadrons were deployed to WestPac. By the following June, 12 fixed wing and 11 helo/observation squadrons were in WestPac. A year later the total was 14 and 13, respectively, and by June 1968 it had risen to 14 and 14, essentially half of the Marine Corps' deployable squadrons.

Except for one or two jet squadrons that would be located in Japan, at any one time all of these squadrons were stationed either in Vietnam or with the Special Landing Force of the Seventh Fleet operating off the coast of Vietnam.

More squadrons could not be deployed because all of the remaining squadrons in the United States were required to train replacements, either for the individual replacement program or for the limited unit rotation program to deploy new aircraft. Other commitments were drastically curtailed or eliminated. For example, no helicopters accompanied the infantry battalions to the Mediterranean. The capabilities of FMFPac and FMFLant to engage in other operations were substantially reduced.

Command, Control, and Coordination
1965–1968

The Marine Corps is proud of the fact that it is a force of combined arms, and it jealously guards the integrity of its air-ground team. Retention of operational control of its air arm is important to the Corps' air-ground team, as air constitutes a significant part of its offensive fire power. Ever since the Korean War, when the 1stMarDiv was under operational control of the Eighth Army and the 1stMAW was under the Fifth Air Force, the Corps has been especially alert to avoid such a split again. It is even more important now because of the increased reliance on helicopters and close air support.

Long before a Marine MEB landed in Vietnam, CinCPac was also concerned about how tactical air operations would be coordinated in the event of a war. Admiral H. D. Felt, who was CinCPac in the early sixties, had studied the lessons of the Korean War and concluded that we needed to do better. And since there was no doctrine upon which all the Services were agreed on that score, he decided to form a board to look into the matter.

Brigadier General McCutcheon was then the assistant chief of staff for operations at CinCPac, and Admiral Felt appointed him to head a twelve-man board with representatives from the CinCPac staff and the three Service component commands. All four Services concerned were represented. The board convened in September 1963 and deliberated for three months. It looked at the full spectrum of tactical air support, which includes five principal functions:

> **Control.** The allocation and management of resources (aircraft and missiles) to achieve maximum effectiveness.
>
> **Antiair warfare.** The destruction of the enemy's air capability in the air and on the ground.
>
> **Offensive air support.** The use of air-to-ground ordnance and other weapon systems in direct and close support at ground troops and in the interdiction of the enemy's rear areas.
>
> **Reconnaissance.** The use of visual, photographic, electronic, and other airborne sensors to acquire information about the enemy and the battlefield environment.
>
> **Transport.** The transportation of men, equipment, and supplies to and from and within the battle area.

The written report of the board contained a number of conclusions. One was that all Services possessed aircraft and that all Services required them in order to carry out their tactical missions. Another was that a joint force commander should appoint one of his Service component commanders to be the coordinating authority for tactical air operations within the area of operations of the joint command.

Admiral Felt neither approved nor disapproved of the board report in its entirety. Nor did his successor, Admiral U. S. Grant Sharp, who relieved him on 1 July 1964. But various recommendations of the report were put into effect by CinCPac in his exercise of overall operational command and management of tactical air resources within the Pacific Command. For example, when photo reconnaissance missions were initiated over Laos in 1964, CinCPac used the coordinating authority technique to coordinate Navy and Air Force reconnaissance efforts. Later on, CinCPac used coordinating authority when air activity was undertaken in Laos and in North Vietnam.

When plans were being made early in 1965 to land Marines at Da Nang, CinCPac informed ComUSMACV that:

> The Commanding General (CG) of the MEB would report to ComUSMACV as Naval Component Commander.
>
> ComUSMACV would exercise operational control of the MEB through the CG of the MEB.
>
> Commander, 2d Air Division, in his capacity as Air Force Component Commander of MACV would act as coordinating authority for matters pertaining to tactical air support and air traffic control in MACV's area of responsibility.

ComUSMACV replied to CinCPac that the Marine jet squadron of the MEB would come under the operational control of his Air Force Component Commander and that such control would be exercised through the tactical air control system. Of course, he added, if the MEB became engaged, it was understood that Marine aircraft would be available for close air support.

The following day CinCPac reiterated his previous guidance to ComUSMACV, namely, that operational control of the squadron would be exercised through the MEB and not the 2d Air Division.

In April 1965, CinCPac promulgated a directive on conduct and control of close air support for the entire Pacific Command, but with emphasis on Vietnam. CinCPac clearly stated that the priority mission in Vietnam was close air support, and the first priority was in support of forces actually engaged with the enemy. The directive went on to say that close air support aircraft would be subject to direct call by the supported ground unit through the medium of the related close air support agency. Among other things, the directive also said that nothing therein vitiated the prior CinCPac position that ComUSMACV'S Air Force Component Commander should act as coordinating authority in matters pertaining to tactical air support and air traffic control.

In June 1965, ComUSMACV initiated a revision of his air support directive, and he drew heavily from the CinCPac Tactical Air Support Board report. The directive was published later that year and revised slightly in 1966, but the pertinent provisions were unchanged.

The MACV directive designated Commander, Seventh Air Force (formerly 2d Air Division), in his capacity as Air Force Component Commander, to act as the coordinating authority for all U.S. and Free World Military Air Force air operations and Vietnamese Air Force activities in the MACV area of operation. Commander, Seventh Air Force, was further given responsibility to establish, in conjunction with U.S. and Vietnamese agencies, an air traffic control system to provide normal processing and flight following. He was also charged to prepare joint instructions, in conjunction with Commanding General, III MAF, and appropriate Army and Navy commanders, to insure integrated and coordinated air operations.

In the same directive, the Commanding General of III MAF was directed to exercise operational control over all Marine Corps aviation resources except in the event of a major emergency or disaster when ComUSMACV might direct Commander, Seventh Air Force, to assume operational control. Commanding General, III MAF, was further enjoined to conduct offensive and defensive tactical air operations to include close air support, interdiction, reconnaissance, maintenance of air superiority, air transport, search and rescue, and other supplemental air support as required. He was also directed to identify to Commander, Seventh Air Force, those resources in excess of current requirements so that such resources could be allocated to support other forces or missions. Finally, he was charged to prepare in conjunction with Commander, Seventh Air Force, joint operating instructions to insure a coordinated and integrated effort.

Concurrently with the revising of the MACV directive, the Commander, Seventh Air Force, Lieutenant General Joseph H. Moore, and the Deputy Commander of III MAF for Air, Brigadier General McCutcheon, were engaged in discussions relative to the degree of control that the Seventh Air Force should have over Marine air assets, particularly with regard to air defense operations. The Air Force desired to have operational control, but the Marines pointed out that the F-4 aircraft was a dual purpose aircraft and that the Marine tactical air control system was used to control all Marine aviation functions, not just air defense. To relinquish operational control would deprive the MAF commander of authoritative direction over one of his major supporting arms.

Nevertheless, the Marines recognized the necessity of having one commander directly responsible for air defense so, after several joint meetings, it was decided to prepare a Memorandum of Agreement which would disseminate basic policies, procedures, and responsibilities. The Air Force was to have overall air defense responsibility and designate an air defense commander. The Commanding General, 1stMAW, was to designate those forces under his command that would participate in air defense, and he agreed that the Air Force would exercise certain authority over those designated resources to include scramble of alert aircraft, designation of targets, declaration of Hawk missile control status, and firing orders. This agreement was signed by the two commanders in August 1965. Overall operational control of Marine air resources was retained under III MAF, but requisite authority for purposes of air defense was passed to the Air Force.

These two documents provided the basic policy for command, control, and coordination of Marine aviation in Vietnam until early 1968, and they were entirely adequate as far as III MAF was concerned.

Single Management (1968–1970)
Late in 1967, the buildup began for the Battle of Khe Sanh. General Westmoreland had directed massive air support for the garrison there, and

both the 1stMAW and Seventh Air Force responded in full. Both General Westmoreland and General William W. Momyer, Commander, Seventh Air Force, believed more effective use could be made of MACV's total air resources if they were managed by a single commander and staff. Early in 1968, a directive was prepared to implement the concept.

The proposed directive required the Commanding General, III MAF, to make available to the Deputy ComUSMACV for Air (who was also Commander, Seventh Air Force) for mission direction all of his strike and reconnaissance aircraft and his tactical air control system as required. The term "mission direction" was not defined. Deputy ComUSMACV for Air was to be responsible for fragging and operational direction of these resources. "Operational direction" was not defined either. "Fragging" is a common aviation term which means to issue a fragmentary order to cover details of a single mission, that is, what is required, where, and when.

The Marines, both in Vietnam and in Washington, objected to the proposed directive on two counts: first, the system as proposed would increase the response time for air support; and second, they reasoned it wasn't necessary.

With regard to the first point, MACV modified the proposed system to improve the response time so that for Marines it wouldn't be any longer than it had been formerly, and for the Army units it would be better. On the second count, MACV remained convinced that it was necessary.

The directive was approved by CinCPac and went into effect in March 1968. The system required the 1stMAW to identify its total sortie capability to Seventh Air Force daily on the basis of a 1.0 sortie rate, that is, one sortie per day for each jet aircraft possessed. Previously the 1stMAW had fragged its aircraft against air support requests received from the Marine ground units, and then identified daily to Seventh Air Force the excess sorties that would be available. These were then fragged by Seventh Air Force on either out-of-country missions or in-country in support of forces other than Marine units. The majority of air support could be forecast and planned in advance except the requirements that might be generated by troops in contact with the enemy. These requirements could be met by extra sorties, scrambles from the hot pad, or by diverting aircraft in the air.

As time went on the participants in the single management system made changes in order to improve efficiency and effectiveness. One such change was the fragging of a portion of the air support on a weekly basis rather than daily. This permitted the more or less standard recurring flights to be handled with less paperwork, while the more routine requests could still be fragged on a daily basis. Seventh Air Force also fragged back to 1stMAW a set number of sorties to take care of unique Marine requirements such as helicopter escort and landing zone preparation which were tied closely to helo operations.

When single management was inaugurated, two new DASCs were added to I Corps. One was established at the III MAF Command Post at Camp Horn, in East Da Nang, and one at the XXIV Corps Command Post at Phu Bai. The one at III MAF was the senior DASC in I Corps and was given authority to scramble strike aircraft without further reference to the Tactical Air Command Center (TACC) in Saigon. This scramble authority was not delegated to similar DASCs in other Corps areas. I Corps was unique in that it was the only Corps area that had both Marine and Air Force tactical air squadrons and both Marine and Army divisions.

Since the 1stMAW generally exceeded the 1.0 sortie rate, all sorties generated in excess of 1.0 could be scrambled by Horn DASC. These excess sorties, plus those fragged back to meet unique Marine requirements, amounted to a sizeable percentage of the 1stMAW's effort, and so, for all practical purposes, the system worked around to just about where it was in the pre-single management days as far as identification or fragging of Marine sorties was concerned.

There is no doubt about whether single management was an overall improvement as far as MACV as a whole was concerned. It was. And there is no denying the fact that, when three Army divisions were assigned to I Corps and interspersed between the two Marine divisions, a higher order of coordination and cooperation was required than previously.

The system worked. Both the Air Force and the Marines saw to that. But the way it was made to work evolved over a period of time, and a lot of it was due to gentlemen's agreements between the on-the-scene commanders. A detailed order explaining the procedures was never published subsequent to the initial directive. The basic MACV directive on air support, however, was revised in 1970 to take into account the advent of single management.

The revised MACV directive defined the term "mission direction" or "operational direction" which had been used in the basic single management directive but not defined. "Mission direction" was stated to be the authority delegated to one commander (i.e., Deputy ComUSMACV for Air) to assign specific air tasks to another commander (i.e., CG III MAF) on a periodic basis as implementation of a basic mission previously assigned by a superior commander (ComUSMACV). In other words, ComUSMACV assigned CG III MAF a basic mission to conduct offensive air support, and ComUSMACV delegated to his Deputy for Air the authority to task CG III MAF for specific missions on a daily and weekly basis in frag orders in order that III MAF assets could support the force as a whole.

Although single management never took operational control of his air resources away from CG III MAF, the Marines were worried that that might be the next step. If so it would be a threat to the air-ground team, and it would recreate the Korean War situation all over again. The new MACV directive allayed their fears on this score. Not only did the definition of "mission direction" spell out the extent of control to be exercised, but the directive clearly stated that CG III MAF would exercise operational control over all his air resources, and that he would conduct offensive and defensive air support missions to include the full spectrum of tactical air support.

In short, the Marines did not relinquish operational control of their resources, MACV as a whole received more effective air support, and III MAF continued to receive responsive air support from its own units. Within the system, III MAF had first claim on its own assets, so most

Marine air missions were in support of Marine ground units and the majority of air support received by Marine ground units was provided by Marine air.

Control

Marine Corps doctrine prescribes that the commander of an air-ground team will have operational control of all his weapons systems and employ them in concert as a force of combined arms to accomplish his mission. The Marine commander exercises this operational control through his normal staff planning process and by means of the Marine Air Command and Control System.

The senior agency in this system is the Tactical Air Command Center (TACC). Because the Seventh Air Force had a TACC in Saigon, the 1stMAW center was called a TADC (Tactical Air Direction Center) as provided for in doctrine. This center was established in June 1965 in the wing compound at Da Nang and it functioned there throughout the war. Continuous improvements were made in its physical appearance, but the tasks performed remained essentially the same. The TADC monitored the employment of all Marine aircraft and allocated the resources to specific missions.

There were two principal agencies subordinate to the TADC. These were the Tactical Air Operations Center (TAOC) and Direct Air Support Centers (DASCs).

The TAOC is the hub of activity for air surveillance and air defense. It is provided for by a Marine Air Control Squadron (MACS).

On a Saturday night in May 1965, Marine Air Control Squadron 9 (MACS-9), based at Atsugi, Japan, and commanded by Lieutenant Colonel Charles I. Westcott, received a telephoned order to have an early warning radar and team ready to deploy by air to Vietnam the next day. Three KC-130s from VMGR-152 were loaded on Sunday and flown to Phu Bai where the team set up and began operating as a northern radar site for the Air Force radar station Panama on Monkey Mountain.

The remainder of the squadron deployed to Chu Lai in the summer and established a manual TAOC. The information from the various radars was plotted by hand on vertical display boards just as had been done during World War II and the Korean War. MACS-7 relieved MACS-9 in place in September 1965.

In June 1967, MACS-4 arrived in Vietnam and replaced the manual system with a modern semi-automated, computer-oriented TAOC which had been developed as part of the Marine Tactical Data System, or MTDS. This system had been under development since the late fifties and was compatible with two similar developments by the Navy: the Navy Tactical Data System (NTDS) for surface operations and the Navy Airborne Tactical Data System (ATDS) for airborne control centers.

In order to make most effective use of this equipment it was decided to emplace it on Monkey Mountain where one of the Hawk missile batteries was located. This required more construction effort to enlarge the site to accommodate both MACS-4 and the Hawks. A considerable area was required for the radars and their antennae and for the sixteen helicopter-transportable huts that comprised the TAOC and the four huts that made up the Tactical Data Communications Central (TDCC).

The TAOC gave the 1stMAW a capability to handle 250 aircraft tracks, friendly and hostile, at one time. In addition, from an air defense point of view, the controllers could handle more than 25 air intercepts simultaneously and the TAOC had a built-in missile data link capability.

A team from the Joint Chiefs of Staff visited Southeast Asia and recommended that steps be taken to link the various Services' air control systems together in that theater. A joint task group was established to work out the technical details.

The TAOC was already operating with the NTDS and ATDS units of the Seventh Fleet in the Gulf of Tonkin. The interface between MTDS and these two systems was the Marine TDCC on Monkey Mountain. The TDCC was the logical candidate, therefore, to become the interface with the Air Force system. One more shelter was required. This provided a special data terminal, or "modem," to convert from computer mode to communications mode. In addition, a new program had to be written for the Marine computer. In layman's terms, the result produced a TDCC which was the equivalent of a language translator in three languages. It could receive either Navy, Marine, or Air Force messages and translate the one received into the other two and pass the translation to the respective centers where they could be displayed. The net result was that air defense and air control data could be passed from Thailand to Da Nang to naval ships in the Tonkin Gulf and vice versa. This interface became fully operational in August 1969 and marked a significant step forward in joint operations.

Whereas the TAOC is the main control center for anti-air warfare and air traffic control, the OASC [Operations Air Support Center] is the main center for direct support of the ground troops. Each Marine division initially had a OASC located together with its organic Fire Support Coordination Center (FSCC). As the 3dMarDiv assumed responsibility for the very sizeable Northern I Corps area, it was necessary to establish a OASC at Phu Bai with the Division Headquarters and one at Dong Ha with Division (Forward). Requests for air support, both fixed and rotary wing, were requested and controlled through these agencies. During certain peak periods a Helicopter Direction Center (HOC) was established with the Regimental Headquarters at Camp Evans, midway between Hue and Quang Tri, and a mini-OASC at Khe Sanh. Information was provided by these facilities to aircraft, on request, relative to artillery fires in progress and major air strikes to enable planes to navigate safely between areas. This information was particularly helpful to helicopters. The wing also had the capability to install an HOC on short notice in a KC-130 to provide an airborne OASC if required. This was done on several operations. An airborne OASC was used whenever a ground operation was launched at such a distance from Da Nang that ordinary ground to air communication would be unreliable. The need for airborne OASCs decreased as bases were built throughout I Corps.

The Marine Air Support Squadron (MASS), which is the parent squadron for the OASC, also contains three mobile Air Support Radar Teams (ASRTs). Each team is equipped with the TPQ-10 radar course directing central which provides the capability to control aircraft in direct air support under conditions of low visibility. MASS-2 arrived in Vietnam in April 1965 from Okinawa, and MASS-3 arrived in October from California. The TPQs were up and operating early in the war.

During the summer of 1965, one TPQ-10 was set up for about six weeks near Pleiku in II Corps to provide air support for Army units operating in that area. Both Marine and Air Force aircraft were directed by it. Within I Corps the TPQs were moved as required to provide optimum coverage, and eventually they were deployed from near the DMZ to Chu Lai.

Lieutenant General Moore of the Seventh Air Force visited 1stMAW and was especially interested in this gear since the Air Force had nothing comparable. Subsequently, the Air Force took some radar bomb scoring equipment and developed it into a ground controlled radar bombing device. It became known as Skyspot. Compared to TPQ-10, it had longer range but less mobility.

The A-4, A-6, and F-4 were all equipped with beacons, and the TPQ radar could track them to almost fifty miles under the best conditions. Knowing the radar-aircraft and the radar-target sides of the triangle, the computer could solve the aircraft-target problem for the particular ordnance to be delivered and the operator could instruct the pilot when to drop. The A-4 was also equipped with a link to the auto pilot which could permit automatic control and drop by the TPQ with the pilot flying hands off. Aircraft without a beacon could be tracked by radar to a distance of about thirty-five miles.

The TPQ-10 was a development based on the MPQ-14 used by the Marines in Korea. Replacement for the TPQ-10, making use of recent technology, is currently under development in a joint venture with the Air Force.

Although not part of the tactical air control system, the Marine Air Traffic Control Units (MATCUs) played a vital role in the control of air traffic. Their mission was terminal traffic control around an air base. They provided approach control, ground controlled approach, and tower facilities. The Corps is authorized one MATCU per jet group and, because of their dispersed operations, two per helo group. In Vietnam, the wing operated MATCUs at Chu Lai and Marble Mountain throughout the war and at Phu Bai, Quang Tri, Dong Ha, Khe Sanh, An Hoa, and Baldy as long as Marine units were operating at those bases. Without those units, air operations during the monsoon season would have been next to impossible.

The TAOC and MATCUs were linked together with communications so that en route traffic handled by the former could be handed off to the latter for approach and landing clearance.

All of this command and control equipment—TACC/TAOC, TAOC, OASC, ASRT, MATCU—is completely mobile and expeditionary by design. It can all be withdrawn from Vietnam (or wherever) and used elsewhere.

Air-Ground Coordination

The CG of the 1stMAW was designated as Deputy CG III MAG (Air) and as such he was the Tactical Air Commander for III MAF.

In Vietnam, from March 1966 when the 1stMarDiv entered the country, until November 1969 when the 3dMarDiv redeployed to Okinawa, there were two Marine divisions in III MAF. The Marine Corps could not deploy another wing for reasons pointed out earlier, but the 1stMAW was reinforced to the limit of the Corps' resources so it could support two reinforced divisions. Two LAAM battalions and two helicopter MAGs were deployed plus one air support squadron for each division.

The wing was short two or three transport helicopter squadrons, but no additional squadrons were available. The available squadrons were managed centrally by the wing in order to get the most out of them.

Although an air support squadron was placed with each division, it became evident that more authority was required at the DASC. This point was made abundantly clear when the two Marine divisions became geographically separated with one or two Army divisions employed between them. When the 3dMarDiv was operating in Northern ICTZ, it was well removed from the 1stMAW Command Post and TADC at Da Nang. The communications were not fast enough to permit command decisions to be made about aviation problems. The 1stMAW solved this problem by assigning an Assistant Wing Commander and a few staff officers to the DASC at the 3dMarDiv Command Post and empowering him to make decisions in the name of the Wing Commander regarding air support. Later, when it wasn't always feasible to have a brigadier general present, a colonel was assigned to each of the division DASCs and they had the same command authority. This arrangement worked well and provided a one-for-one relationship, air-to-ground, particularly in the vital area of helicopter support. Coordination was vastly improved.

Employment
Anti-Air Warfare Operations
Vietnam, at least as far as the war in the south was concerned, was not a fighter pilot's war. There were no air-to-air engagements for Marine squadrons. No aces.

But there was a possible threat. So there had to be an air defense system and capability, and it was exercised under the terms of the agreement signed by Generals Moore and McCutcheon. The Marines provided two battalions of Hawk surface-to-air missiles for close-in defense at Da Nang and Chu Lai, F-4 Phantoms on hot pad alert, and an early warning and control capability through its air control squadron.

The Marine LAAM battalion is part of the overall anti-air warfare function. Its principal role is in close-in air defense. The battalion is normally a subordinate unit of the Marine Air Control Group, because in actual operations it is linked to the TAOC which provides information on friendly and enemy air traffic. The TAOC also normally gives "commence" and "cease" fire orders to the missiles.

One LAAM battery arrived in Vietnam in February 1965 and took position on the airfield at Da Nang. Subsequently it moved to Hill 327 west of the field. The two other firing batteries of the battalion eventually were placed on Monkey Mountain east of Da Nang, and in the Hai Van Pass to the north. Part of one of the batteries, known as an assault fire unit, was emplaced on Hill 55 eight miles south of the Da Nang vital area. The best defense of the installations at Da Nang would call for five battery sites, but adequate real estate did not become available until months later.

The 2d LAAM Battalion landed at Chu Lai in September 1965, and set up its firing batteries north and south of the SATS airfield. There were no elevated positions, but this posed a problem for any potential attacker as well.

Although neither battalion fired in anger, they did conduct live practice firings annually in order to keep their state of training high. In addition to firing at radio controlled drones, they fired at targets towed by manned fighter planes.

Offensive Air Support Operations

The main employment of Marine jets was in the delivery of air-to-ground ordnance in direct and close support of ground troops.

In this connection there were some local rules of engagement which had developed over the years, influencing the tactics and techniques to be employed. With very few exceptions, all air strikes had to be controlled by an airborne controller, and most had to have a political as well as a tactical clearance. There was good reason for this. The population was spread out over a considerable area along the coastal region and the U.S. and Vietnamese ground units were operating mainly in the same area. This led to the employment of Forward Air Controllers (Airborne) (FAC[A]). Thus, in a departure from prewar practice, the role of the FAC on the ground was minimized as far as control of air strikes was concerned. However, he had other useful employment.

The O-1 aircraft was used initially for this purpose. The Marine O-1s that were brought into Vietnam were rapidly approaching the end of their service lives, however, and on 1 September 1965, the Marine Corps stopped using them. The OV-10A, which was scheduled to replace them, did not become available until July 1968. To partially alleviate this situation, Headquarters Marine Corps and the Naval Air Systems Command managed to locate about a dozen old O-1s and had them overhauled and airlifted to Vietnam. These were too few, however, so the Marines had to rely on Army observation aircraft and Air Force FAC(A)s for those tactical air control missions demanding an airborne controller. The Air Force used the O-1 initially and later the OV-10A and the Cessna O-2. The latter is a small twin-engine, light aircraft with the engines in line. The one in front drives a tractor propeller and the one in the rear a pusher prop.

In addition to FAC(A)s, the Marine Corps employed Tactical Air Coordinators (Airborne) or TAC(A)s. Whereas FAC(A)s flew low performance aircraft and operated over friendly terrain and within range of artillery support, the TAC(A)s flew high performance jets and operated over territory controlled by the enemy. Their mission was to coordinate various strike aircraft and to ensure they hit the correct targets. In this role the Marines first used the two-seat F-9, but beginning in late 1967 they employed the two-seat TA-4F. These aircraft provided two sets of "eyeballs" rather than one and gave the TAC(A) an increased visual observation capability. The jet performance added a higher degree of survivability to the mission.

The Corps removed one of the two FACs it had in each infantry battalion because of the few opportunities offered them to control strikes and because their aeronautical talent could better be used elsewhere. The one remaining FAC plus the Air Liaison Officer, both aviation officers, continued to carry out their other responsibilities, which included advising their battalion commander on the employment of air support, requesting such support, and controlling helo operations and helo landing zones. This became big business in Vietnam. When the opportunity presented itself, the FAC did control air strikes from the ground. The arrival of the A-6 aircraft in Vietnam introduced an advanced avionics weapon system. This system was further improved, as far as close air support is concerned, when the Marines deployed small radar beacons for use with their ground FACs. With this beacon, known as RABFAC, a FAC's precise position on the ground could be displayed on the radar scope in an A-6. The FAC could provide the bearing and distance of the target from the beacon, plus the elevation difference between the two, and the bombardier-navigator in the A-6 could enter this data into the weapon system computer, and bomb the target in bad weather or at night with accuracies approaching that of A-4s in clear, daylight deliveries.

The A-6 aircraft displayed great versatility and lived up to the expectations of those who pushed its development after the Korean War. It is the only operational aircraft that has a self-contained all-weather bombing capability including a moving target indicator mode. In this role it was used rather extensively in the monsoon season, not only in South Vietnam but also in Laos and over the heavily defended area of North Vietnam. The usual bomb load was 14,000 pounds.

Both the A-4 and F-4 were used in offensive air support with great success. The average bomb load for the A-4 was about 3,000 pounds, and for the F-4 about 5,000 pounds. These aircraft were generally fragged against planned missions, but they could also be scrambled from the alert pad, or they could be diverted in flight to higher priority targets.

The F-8 was also used during the period December 1965 through May 1968. It was in the process of being replaced in the Marine inventory by the F-4, but while it was in Vietnam it did a fine job in air-to-ground missions.

The F-8 was also the only Marine strike aircraft to be based on board a carrier of the Seventh Fleet during the Vietnam War. Marine All-Weather

Fighter Squadron 212 (VMF[AW]-212), commanded by Lieutenant Colonel Charles H. Ludden, was embarked in the attack carrier USS *Oriskany* (CVA-34) in 1965 when she was operating off Vietnam. The squadron pilots were trained as fighter pilots but, when the carrier arrived in the Gulf of Tonkin, the urgent need was for attack aircraft which could deliver bombs. The primary mission of VMF(AW)-212 became the attack of ground targets, and the squadron flew strikes in North and South Vietnam. Both the Navy and Marine Corps would have liked to have had more Marine squadrons afloat, but if they had been afloat, they wouldn't have been ashore and the Corps couldn't do both. Now that we have cut force levels in Vietnam, the Marine Corps has once again deployed aviation units aboard carriers.

During 1965, and into the early part of 1966, there was a shortage of aviation ordnance. Time was required to set up production lines in the United States and get the pipeline filled all the way to Vietnam. In the meantime, the 1stMAW used what was available in contingency stocks, and this included a great number of old high drag "fat" bombs. The old bombs had a much larger cross section than the new ones, hence they added drag to the aircraft and reduced its speed and radius of action. Again because of their cross section, fewer of the old bombs could be loaded on multiple bomb racks. The wing never lost a sortie because of ordnance, but it did have to substitute items on occasion because the preferred store was not available. In order to husband its resources, the wing commander issued a message directing that if ordnance could not be dropped on a worthwhile target, it would be brought back to base, not jettisoned.

By late 1966, a wide range of ordnance was available, including 250, 500, 1,000, and 2,000-pound bombs; 2.75 inch and five-inch rockets; napalm; 20mm. cannon; smoke; and certain other stores for special targets. There is still a requirement, however, for better aviation weapons. We need to get better first pass accuracy to reduce the number of passes over the target. One promising way to improve effectiveness appears to be offered by lasers.

Up to April 1966, ComUSMACV was not involved in the air war in North Vietnam. That war was conducted by the Commander-in-Chief, Pacific Fleet (CinCPacFlt), and Commander-in-Chief, Pacific Air Force (CinCPacAF). 1stMAW electronic EF-10Bs flew missions in the north before this, but they did so in support of the Seventh Fleet or the Seventh Air Force as subordinates of PacFlt and PacAF. On 1 April 1966, Com-USMACV was authorized by CinCPac to conduct air strikes in, and to the north of, the DMZ in what was known as Route Package One. By summer, Marine aircraft were assigned to strike there against artillery and rocket sites as well as other military targets.

With the addition of the A-6A to its inventory, the 1stMAW had the finest all-weather bombing aircraft in the world. Late in 1966, A-6s began striking targets as far north as Hanoi and Haiphong—and carried on until the bombing halt in 1968, striking mostly at night. North Vietnam was, of course, heavily defended with antiaircraft artillery and surface-to-air missiles. EA-6As provided electronic jamming in support of the strike birds, and Marine F-4Bs flew cover for them to keep MIGs off their backs. Additionally, the two Marine A-6 squadrons flew strikes in other route packages as directed.

Reconnaissance Operations

As noted earlier, VMCJ-1 was one of the first fixed-wing squadrons to deploy to Vietnam. In more than five years of continuous operations from Da Nang, the squadron made major contributions in the field of electronic warfare and imagery reconnaissance.

During the opening phases of the air war against North Vietnam, the EF-10Bs of VMCJ-1 were the only jet tactical electronic warfare aircraft available to provide support for U.S. Air Force and Navy strikes. To meet the requirements levied on the squadron, active electronic countermeasures were emphasized. Electronic reconnaissance was conducted en route to and from the target. In the target area, jamming occupied most of the electronic countermeasure operators' attention. In July 1965, U.S. Air

Force aircraft conducted the first strikes in history against surface-to-air missile (SAM) sites. Six EF-10Bs from VMCJ-1 supported the strike. There was no loss of aircraft to radar controlled weapons. The Navy also had an electronic warfare capability, but its EKA-3 was a combination tanker-electronic warfare aircraft and was limited to standoff jamming as opposed to close-in jamming in company with the strike aircraft. The Navy also had some EA-1s, but these were propeller-driven aircraft and were not able to keep up with the jets, hence, they too were used in a standoff role. The Air Force effort in electronic warfare was devoted almost exclusively to larger aircraft and in a "strategic," rather than a tactical, role. After the war in Vietnam got underway, they did modify some B-66 aircraft to the electronic mission.

In November 1966, the EA-6A made its debut in the theater. The quantum increase in electronic warfare capability represented by the EA-6A came in the nick of time. The cancerous spread of SAMs throughout North Vietnam made an eventual confrontation between Marine attack aircraft and SAMs inevitable. In April 1967, a Marine A-4 was shot down by a SAM from a site located in the DMZ. In response to the new threat, EF-10Bs began a continual patrol along the DMZ during hours of darkness when the SAMs were prone to fire. The more sophisticated EA-6As provided electronic warfare support for missions against targets located in the high threat areas of the north. Because of the need for electronic warfare aircraft, it was not until 1969 that the old EF-10Bs were at last able to leave Vietnam. As of this writing the EA-6A is the only tactical electronic warfare aircraft in any Service that can accompany strike aircraft to the target and maneuver with them.

In the relatively new art of electronic warfare, aircraft from VMCJ-1 performed in every role: escort for B-52s, support for tactical air strikes, and as intelligence collectors. Lessons learned were documented, tactics became more sophisticated, and hardware was evolved to increase the effectiveness of the electronic warfare capability.

The other side of the VMCJ-1 house, imagery reconnaissance, was equally engaged. Collection of imagery intelligence in the fight against the hard-to-locate enemy of the south varied to a great degree from flights over relatively well defined targets in the north. In the south, the usual imagery reconnaissance mission produced evidence of enemy activity, but the enemy was seldom pinpointed. To determine enemy intentions, reconnaissance flights over the same areas were conducted periodically. Interpreters then looked for telltale indications of change or deviations from the norm that had been established by previous flights. With the RF-8A, the imagery coverage of large areas required by this type of intelligence determination was confined to periods of daylight hours and relatively good weather. Replacement of the RF-8A with multi-sensor RF-4B aircraft, beginning in October 1966, provided VMCJ-1 with an around-the-clock collection capacity. As experience was gained with the new systems, night infrared reconnaissance played an ever increasing role in the overall intelligence collection effort.

TA-4Fs flew hundreds of missions in the Route Package One area of North Vietnam, performing in the visual reconnaissance as well as in the TAC(A) role. They located SAM sites, truck parks, supply dumps, and other targets, and then controlled other strike aircraft against them. They also spotted and controlled naval gunfire for the USS *New Jersey* (BB-62) and other ships that participated in bombarding the north.

Visual reconnaissance by low performance aircraft is still an absolute necessity. Maneuverable, fixed-wing aircraft still have a place in this role, and the OV-10A performed better than expected. However, there is a requirement for a quieter aircraft that can overfly targets without being detected. Had such an aircraft been available, it could have been used very profitably to patrol the rocket belt around the vital area of Da Nang. There is a prototype aircraft designated the YO-3 that gives promise of this capability, but the Marine Corps does not have any.

Fixed-Wing Transport Operations
Marine transports and helos were not included under single management. The Marines had two models of fixed-wing transports in Vietnam, the

venerable C-117 and the work-horse KC-130. The former was assigned only in small numbers, one per group, and was used for organic logistic support. It became apparent in 1965, however, that there were some voids in the Marine capability as far as aircraft were concerned, so the C-117s were rapidly drafted to fill some of these. Examples were flare drops, radio relay, and use as an airborne control center. Later on, US-2Bs and C-1As were assigned to the wing, and sometimes they were also used for some of these tasks.

Marine Refueler Transport Squadron 152 (VMGR-152) was based in Japan when the war began, but it moved to Okinawa late in 1965. It kept a four (or more) plane detachment at Da Nang. This little detachment did everything imaginable as far as air transport was concerned. It hauled men and equipment between major bases in Vietnam and to outposts such as Khe Sanh that had suitable airstrips, and it air-dropped to those that did not. It provided aerial refueler service for Marine jets, particularly those that operated up north. In 1965, whenever the strip at Chu Lai was less than eight thousand feet and A-4s were required to take off with reduced fuel loads, there was a KC-130 tanker in orbit to tank them after climb-out. These Hercules also served as airborne direct air support centers and as flare ships. They were a reliable and versatile transport.

The KC-130 is getting on in years, however, and in spite of the fact that it was retrofitted with larger engines, the aircraft is only marginally capable of refueling a loaded A-6 or F-4 in flight. Furthermore, a considerable number of them are required to provide refueling service for a fighter squadron ferrying across the Pacific. Because they can't get to the same altitude as the jets, the jets have to descend to receive fuel. This requires blocking off a lot of airspace and frequently this is a constraint on a long trans-oceanic ferrying operation since it interferes with commercial flights.

What the Corps needs is a transport like the C-141, modified to be similar in capability to the KC-130.

The Corps also needs a replacement for the obsolete C-117s and those C-54s still on hand. It is willing to accept a smaller number of more modern aircraft to carry out the missions that are not applicable for the KC-130 or 141. A combination of T-39s and something like the Fairchild-Hiller F-227 would give the Corps a modern high-speed passenger and cargo hauling capability.

Helicopter Operations

Vietnam was certainly a helicopter war for U.S. forces. It is difficult to envisage how we would have fought there without them.

After years of study and development, the Marine Corps pioneered the use of helicopters in ground warfare in Korea. In the following years it planned to build up its force, and simultaneously it pursued the development of more capable aircraft. The Corps' basic requirement was for adequate helicopter lift to execute the ship-to-shore movement in an amphibious operation. To do this two basic transport helicopters were decided on, one for medium lift and one for heavy lift.

Although the Corps was authorized eighteen permanent transport helicopter squadrons and two temporary ones for Southeast Asia, it only deployed ten to the Western Pacific. The remaining nine (one temporary one was never formed because of lack of resources) were required to remain in the United States to train replacement pilots for the overseas pipeline. Additional squadrons could not be deployed because they could not be supported. The deployment of even one more would have upset the delicate balance of replacement training versus overseas requirements.

As part of the planning, programming, and budgeting cycle that takes place annually in Washington in each of the Services and in the Office of the Secretary of Defense, the Marine Corps accepted a change in its transport helicopter mix, from fifteen medium and three heavy to twelve medium and six heavy. With the one temporary squadron added, this gave thirteen and six. Eventually seven of the mediums and three of the heavies were stationed overseas.

The transition from the UH-34 and CH-37 to the CH-46 and CH-53, respectively, represented a major increase in capability, but, at the same time, there were problems involving acceptance of the new models, shaking them down, training pilots and maintenance personnel, developing techniques and procedures, and establishing an adequate supply posture.

Squadrons equipped with the twelve-year-old UH-34 bore the brunt of helo operations in 1965 and for well over a year thereafter. CH-46s began to arrive in Vietnam in March 1966, when Lieutenant Colonel Warren C. Watson's HMM-164 flew to Marble Mountain from the USS *Valley Forge* (LPH-8). It was not until 1969 that all UH-34s were withdrawn. On 18 August, the blades of the last UH-34 were folded, thus marking the end of an era for Marine Corps helicopters in Vietnam. The UH-34 had performed for over seven years there in an outstanding manner.

A detachment of obsolescent CH-37s arrived from Santa Ana, California, in the summer of 1965 and did yeoman service pending arrival of the CH-53 in January 1967, when Major William R. Beeler brought in a four-plane detachment from HMH-463. By the end of the year there were two full squadrons of CH-53s in Vietnam.

In Vietnam there were several technical problems that had an impact on helicopter employment. First of all, the tropical environment reduced payload because of characteristically high temperatures and humidity. Second, the sandy and dusty landing zones created extensive maintenance problems, particularly for engines. Filters had to be developed for all helos to reduce the amount of foreign particles that were being ingested into the air inlets. These filters increased aircraft weight and lowered engine thrust by a few per cent. Third, there was a requirement to install additional armor in all helos to protect their vital parts against the ever increasing enemy antiaircraft fire. Finally, the addition of armament and gunners naturally reduced proportionately what could be carried.

As a matter of necessity the transports were armed with door guns. The UH-34s could only take the 7.62-mm. machine gun, and two of these with a gunner (the crew chief manned one gun) reduced the troop carrying capacity by two men. The CH-46 and -53 helos were able to carry

.50 caliber machine guns, one on each side, and although their loads were reduced too, the reduction, particularly in the case of the CH-53, was not so noticeable.

During the period October 1966 through October 1967, the CH-46 experienced a series of catastrophic accidents which caused the Corps and the Naval Air Systems Command to take a hard look at the design of the aircraft. These accidents occurred in the United States as well as Vietnam and in most cases involved failure of the aircraft's rear pylon. A program was initiated to strengthen that section of the airframe, and it was accomplished in two phases. The first improvement was incorporated in Okinawa for Vietnam-based aircraft. The second phase was performed later at overhaul. The modification program had an impact on helo operations in Vietnam because fewer were available for combat operations. To partially offset this shortage, some UH-34s were airlifted to Da Nang from Cherry Point, North Carolina, in Military Airlift Command transports. Following the modification program, the CH-46 performed in an outstanding manner.

The Marine Corps experimented with armed helicopters as early as 1950, but it did not pursue an active program for several reasons. The transport helicopters in the inventory before the war began in Vietnam were limited in payload to begin with, and the Corps chose to devote their full load capacity to carrying men and equipment, while relying on attack aircraft to escort the helicopters. At the same time, it sought to procure a light helicopter which could perform a myriad of tasks, including the role of a gunship. This program was a long time in materializing, but it finally resulted in the UH-1E. The Army, on the other hand, with no fixed wing attack aircraft, depended heavily on "gun birds."

One gunship version of the Marine UH-IE was armed with a nose turret which could be elevated, depressed, and swung left and right. In addition, weight permitting, it could mount left and right fixed, forward-firing machine guns, or 2.75 inch rocket pods. A .30 caliber machine gun could also be installed in each of the two side doors.

The helo gunship proved to be indispensable. It was more immediately available than jets, more maneuverable, and it could work close-in with transport helicopters.

The UH-1E has been used by the Marines since 1965 to perform many tasks. They include serving as gunships; as command and control craft for MAF division, wing, regimental, and occasionally battalion commanders; for liaison, courier, and administrative runs; for visual reconnaissance and observation; as aerial searchlights when special equipment was installed; as platforms for various kinds of sensors; as transportation for VIPs (and this was no small order); for medical evacuation of casualties; and for miscellaneous roles.

In 1965, the Corps was authorized 12 light helos per wing, and these were included in each of the three VMO [Marine observation] squadrons. Two additional VMOs were authorized for the war in Southeast Asia and in 1968 the Department of Defense authorized the Marine Corps to convert them to three light helicopter transport squadrons (HML), giving the Corps three VMOs and three HMLs. The VMOs were to have 18 OV-10As and 12 light helos each, and the HMLs were to have 24 light helos. Two of each kind of squadron were on hand in the 1stMAW by the latter part of 1968. This provided 72 light helos (including gunships) to support two reinforced divisions, but it still was not enough to meet all of the requirements. If there is any lesson that has been learned in Vietnam, it is that the Corps needs more light helicopters. The statistics accumulated over the past several years indicate that on the basis of hours of use there is a requirement for these aircraft nearly equal to the combined total of medium and heavy helicopters.

The AH-1G Cobra was not available for Marine use until April 1969. The gunship was accepted with enthusiasm by the *pilots*, performed well in a fire suppression role, and was maintained at a rather high rate of availability. Organizationally, they might be in a VMO or an HML. Ideally, 24 of them would form an HMA, one in each wing.

The Corps has under procurement twin-engine versions of both the UH-1 and the AH-1, and these should be major improvements over the current single-engine configurations. The benefits will be increased payload capability under a wider range of temperatures and altitudes, and the added reliability provided by having a second power plant. The twin Cobra was due to enter the force in 1970 and the twin UH-1 in 1971.

The first UH-34 squadrons were employed in much the same way as they had been during the "Shufly" years. They lifted troops and cargo on either tactical or administrative missions and performed the usual spectrum of miscellaneous tasks. They conducted the first night assault in Vietnam in August 1965. The 2d battalion, 3d Marines, was lifted into Elephant Valley, northwest of Da Nang.

By the end of 1965, Marine transport helos were lifting an average of 40,000 passengers and over 2,000 tons of cargo a month while operating from their main bases at Ky Ha and Marble Mountain.

In 1968, the helicopters carried an average of over 50,000 men and over 6,000 tons of cargo a month. This increase in capacity was due mainly to the substitution of CH-46 helos for UH-34s between 1966 and 1968. The increase in the requirement came mainly because of heavy assault operations against North Vietnamese Army divisions which had invaded the I Corps Tactical Zone. And in the first half of 1970, even after redeployment had commenced, they were lifting more than 70,000 passengers and 5,000 tons of cargo in a month. Part of this increase can be attributed to the increased use of the CH-53 in troop lifts.

Even back in "Shufly" days, Marine helicopter pilots learned to expect all sorts of strange cargo on the manifest. They often had to move Vietnamese units, and this included dependents and possessions, cows and pigs included.

As larger transports entered service, larger loads were carried. And this of course included larger animals. HMH-463 with its CH-53s was tasked to move a remotely located Vietnamese camp. Included in the lift requirement were two elephants. Not big ones, but nevertheless elephants. These pachyderms were tranquilized and carried externally with no problem. The crews named them "Ev" and "Charlie," which proves that they had found some time to read the newspapers sent out from home.

With the CH-53, the 1stMAW could retrieve battle damaged UH-1s, UH-34s, and CH-46s that might otherwise have been destroyed. The CH-53 could not lift another 53, however, under operating conditions in Vietnam. There is a need for a small number of heavy lift helicopters that can retrieve all helicopters and all tactical fixed-wing aircraft except transports. Such a heavy lift helicopter would also be useful in lifting heavy engineering equipment and other loads beyond the capability of the CH-53. The Army's CH-54 Skycrane's lifting capability is not sufficiently greater to make it a really attractive choice. A payload of at least 18 tons is required. Furthermore, the helicopter should be compatible with shipboard operations, and it should be capable of being disassembled and transported in C-5A or C-141 cargo planes.

One of the most hazardous helicopter missions was the evacuation of casualties at night or in poor weather. The problem was twofold: finding the correct zone, and getting in and out without getting shot up. Since most medevacs were called in by troops in contact with the enemy, the available landing zones had no landing aides to help the pilot, and so he had to rely on an accurate designation and visual identification or confirmation. At night a flare aircraft was often required to orbit the area and illuminate the zone so it could be positively identified. Gunships or jets would provide fire suppression, if required, and the evacuation helo would make a fast approach and retirement, making maximum use of whatever natural concealment might be available.

There is no doubt about it, the helicopter saved countless lives in Vietnam. If the casualty could be evacuated to a medical facility in short order, his chances of survival were very good.

Although a small number of helos were fragged each day specifically for medical evacuation, any helicopter in the air was available for such a mission, if required, and many evacs were made by on-the-scene aircraft. These helicopters of course did not carry hospital corpsmen as did those specifically fragged for the mission, but they offered the advantage of being closer, and thus quicker to respond.

The number of medevac missions flown by Marine helicopters is large indeed—in the peak year of 1968, nearly 67,000 people were evacuated in just short of 42,000 sorties—and a great many of the helos sustained hits and casualties themselves in the process of flying these missions. As a group, helicopter crews were awarded a very high percentage of Purple Hearts for wounds received in combat. They were and are very courageous men.

Multi-Function Operations

The majority of operations conducted by III MAF required some degree of air support, and in most cases the support involved two or more tactical air functions. A complete recounting of all these operations is beyond the scope of this article. However, some representative examples are in order so that the reader may appreciate the role of Marine air in MAF operations.

As the MAF units began to undertake offensive operations, helicopters were essential for troop transport and logistic resupply, and jets were equally important for close air support. Operation Double Eagle in late January and early February 1966 illustrates several techniques and tactics that were used quite frequently in later operations. This was a multi-battalion force commanded by the Assistant Division Commander of the 3dMarDiv, Brigadier General Jonas M. Platt. The operational area was southern I Corps. Coordination was required with Vietnamese Army units in I Corps and with U.S. Army units in II Corps, specifically the 1st Air Cavalry Division. One Marine battalion and helo squadron belonged to the SLF and were embarked in the USS *Valley Forge* and other ships of the Amphibious Ready Group. MAG-36 was placed in direct support of Platt's Task Force Delta. Colonel William G. Johnson, Commanding Officer of MAG-36, located his command post adjacent to Platt's. He also established a helicopter operating area with limited maintenance support. This became known as "Johnson City." Logistic support was added: fuel, ammunition, supplies, and a medical aid station. This was in effect a Logistic Support Area (LSA), and it was essential to establish one in order to support mobile ground operations such as those in which General Platt was engaged. As the war progressed, these LSAs would become strategically located throughout the Corps area and close to main roads so that the bulk of supplies could be brought in by truck convoys. If an airfield were near, fixed-wing transport could be used. MAG-36 and Task Force Delta had a mini-DASC located at "Johnson City" through which they could control aircraft assigned to them. Helicopters were immediately available through Colonel Johnson. Jets had to be requested, but the route was direct to the TADC which could scramble A-4s from Chu Lai or F-4s from Da Nang.

Major General McCutcheon was relieved as CG 1stMAW by Major General Louis B. Robertshaw on 15 May 1966. The Struggle Movement within South Vietnam which led to the establishment of the Ky government in Saigon was still unresolved at this point, and an upsurge of political activity forced the cancellation of the planned change-of-command ceremonies. A small impromptu one was held outside III MAF Headquarters.

During General Robertshaw's tenure, the center of action tended to shift north, both on the ground and in the air. In July and August 1966, Operation Hastings produced the highest number of enemy killed to date. The Prairie series of operations, which began shortly thereafter, took place in the same locale, just south of the DMZ. Names like Dong Ha, the "Rockpile," and Con Thien came into prominence. But there was another name which was destined to become even more prominent, Khe Sanh. Late in April 1967, a Marine company made solid contact with North Vietnamese regulars northwest of Khe Sanh. On the 25th, the 3d Battalion of the 3d Marines was helo-lifted into Khe Sanh, and the next day the SLF battalion (2d Battalion, 3d Marines) was heloed into Phu Bai and thence lifted by KC-130 to Khe Sanh. Both battalions took the offensive and attacked the enemy on Hills 881 South and North. In two weeks of bitter fighting, the 1stMAW flew over one thousand sorties in around-the-clock close and direct air support of Marine infantry in the area. Here was an example of the integrated employment of fixed- and rotary-wing transports, close air support, and air control.

Major General Norman J. Anderson relieved Robertshaw on 2 June 1967. His tour was marked with a further buildup of North Vietnamese forces in Northern I Corps and the introduction of single management. The enemy's Tet offensive of 1968, the battle of Hue, and the campaign of Khe Sanh all occurred on his watch. During the Khe Sanh campaign, the entire spectrum of tactical air support was called into play—not only Marine, but also Air Force, Navy, and Vietnamese Air Force. And SAC's [Strategic Air Command's] B-52s dropped their heavy loads upon the enemy in the surrounding hills.

One example of how all Marine tactical air functions could be coordinated into a single operational mission was the "Super Gaggle." This was a technique developed by the 1stMAW to resupply the hill outposts in the vicinity of Khe Sanh. These hills were surrounded with heavy concentrations of enemy antiaircraft weapons, and every flight by a helo into one of the outposts was an extremely hazardous mission. Additionally, the weather in February was typically monsoon, and flying was often done on instruments. The "Super Gaggle" was a flight of transport helos escorted by A-4 jets and UH-1E gunships, all under the control of a TAC(A) in a TA-4F. The key was to take advantage of any break in the weather and to have all aircraft rendezvous over the designated point at the same time.

The operation was usually scrambled at the request of the mini-DASC at Khe Sanh on the basis that a break in the weather was expected shortly. The TAC(A) and KC-130 tankers took off from Da Nang, the A-4s from Chu Lai, UH-1E gunships from Quang Tri and CH-46s from Dong Ha. All aircraft rendezvoused over Khe Sanh within a 30 minute period under control of the TAC(A). Instrument climb-outs were often required due to weather. Even the CH-46s with external loads would climb out on a tacan bearing until they were on top. Under direction of the TAC(A), and taking advantage of the break in the clouds if it did develop, the area was worked over with napalm, rockets, 20-mm., and smoke. The CH-46s let down in a spiral column and deposited their loads on Khe Sanh and the hill outposts in less than five minutes and then spiraled back on top and returned to their bases. The jets also climbed back on top, plugged in to the KC-130 tankers for refueling, and headed back to Da Nang and Chu Lai.

The fourth commander of the 1stMAW was Major General Charles J. Quilter. He relieved Anderson on 19 June 1968. His tour saw a reversal of the trend that started in General Robertshaw's era. The enemy withdrew after taking severe beatings at Khe Sanh, Hue, and elsewhere in ICTZ. The enemy gave up conventional large scale operations and reverted to the strategy of small unit actions and harassment.

III MAF forces underwent an operational change too. Once the 3dMarDiv was relieved of the requirement for a static defense along the strong-point barrier, they were free to undertake a mobile offensive in Northern ICTZ and strike at the enemy in the western reaches. One of the finest examples of air-ground teamwork took place during the period of January through March 1969. The code name of the operation was Dewey Canyon. The locale was the upper A Shau Valley and southern Da Krong Valley. This was a multi-battalion operation involving the 9th Marine Regiment, commanded by Colonel Robert H. Barrow, and two battalions of the 1st Vietnamese Army Division.

During the last week of the pre–Dewey Canyon period, Marine attack and fighter-attack aircraft from MAGs 11, 12, and 13 flew 266 sorties over the objective area, dropping over 730 tons of ordnance.

On 21 January, D-1, a "Zippo" team, was formed of representatives of the 1stMAW and 3dMarDiv. Infantry, engineer, helicopter, and observation aircraft specialists were included. This team was responsible to the overall ground commander for landing zone and fire support; base selection and preparation; and coordination of the helicopter assault.

Early on D-Day the initial landing zones (LZ) were prepared by fixed wing air strikes (made suitable for helo landings by bombing and strafing to reduce threat of opposition to a minimum), and elements of the 2d Battalion, 9th Marines, landed at 0800. In the rapid buildup that followed, CH-46s, under the control of the division DASC and under the protective umbrella of gunships and observation aircraft, brought 1,544 Marines and 46 tons of cargo into two LZs. By the evening of 24 January, a battery of 105-mm. howitzers from the 2d Battalion, 12th Marines, and the Command Post of the 9th Marines were in place on one of these landing zones, which became known as RAZOR.

The following day, three companies of the 3d Battalion were helolifted on to a ridgeline further forward, known as Co Ka Va. It would soon be developed into Fire Support Base (FSB) Cunningham, named for the first Marine aviator. In a few more days, elements of the 2d Battalion from FSB Riley pushed down the ridgeline to establish another FSB, Dallas, to guard the western approach to the area from Laos. To the east, the two Vietnamese battalions were lifted into two other bases. They would secure the left flank and cut off the enemy escape route to the east.

About the 1st of February, the "Crachin" season really began to make itself felt. This is a period when low clouds and drizzle cover the mountain tops in Northern I Corps and obscure visibility in the valleys.

On 4 February, a company of the 3d Battalion moved into and occupied what was to become the last FSB for the coming infantry advance. Erskine was to be its name.

Marine helicopters continually worked out of FSB Vandegrift carrying essential supplies of ammunition, rations, and water to the various bases. On the return trips they carried wounded back to aid stations. Often the weather precluded access to the area except by flying on instruments. Under such conditions, over 40 pallets of critically needed supplies were dropped by KC-130s and CH-46s under control of the TPQ-10 at Vandegrift.

When artillery was in place on both Cunningham and Erskine, the 9th Marines began moving on foot from their bases into the Da Krong Valley with battalions on line. Their objective was Tiger Mountain and the ridgeline that ran west from it. As they advanced, landing zones were carved out of the jungle with 2,000-pound bombs or, as a minimum, sufficient space was created so that a medevac could be performed by helo hoist, or an external load could be dropped to the troops on the ground.

On 17 February, Marine helicopter resupply during instrument conditions received its biggest boost. Instrument departure and return corridors were established to permit loaded helos to operate out of Quang Tri in support of the operation. The technique was the same as that employed during Khe Sanh operations. During the next month of corridor operation, over 2,000 Marine aircraft were funneled in and out of this highway in the sky to keep Dewey Canyon alive.

Other elements of the air component continued to seek out the enemy and to attack him. O-1, RF-4, EA-6, A-4, F-4, and A-6 aircraft all participated. And when emergency missions arose during darkness, OV-10A, C-117, or KC-130 aircraft were called in to provide illumination by dropping flares.

The 22nd of February saw the lead element of the 3d Battalion gain the crest of Tiger Mountain. In a few days it became FSB Turnage.

The 24th found the 1st Battalion in possession of the enemy's headquarters at Tam Boi. The 2d Battalion took control of the ridgeline overlooking Route 922, where it crosses from Vietnam into Laos.

The 27th marked the first time a TPQ-10 had ever been emplaced and operated from an FSB. One was placed on Cunningham and remained there for 17 days, controlling 72 air strikes, ten A-6 beacon drops, and three emergency paradrops.

The days that followed turned up masses of enemy equipment and stores, and the quantity accumulated and sent back to our bases was easily the largest amount yet discovered during the war.

The 18th of March marked the final day of operation of Dewey Canyon. On this day virtually the entire resources of the 1stMAW were committed. Over 350 tons of cargo and 1,400 Marines were helo-lifted out of Turnage and Tam Boi without a casualty. These were the last two bases to be vacated. Gunships and jets flew close cover and close air support.

Perhaps the most notable accomplishment of the operation was that only one helicopter was lost in spite of the adverse weather and terrain and the efforts of a stubborn, well-trained, and professional enemy to counter the operation. Lieutenant General Richard G. Stilwell, U.S. Army, commander of all U.S. ground forces in Northern I Corps under CG III MAP, summed it up in a few words when he said, "Dewey Canyon deserves some space in American military history by sole reason of audacity, guts, and team play. I cannot applaud too highly the airmen of the 1stMAW in a variety of roles."

General Quilter was relieved by Major General William G. Thrash on 7 July 1969. Thrash took command when the wing was at its maximum strength and operating a peak number of facilities. The wing was supporting two Army divisions, two ARVN divisions (splitting the helo load with Army helicopters), and the Korean Marine Brigade, in addition to the two Marine divisions. It also flew out-of-country missions. Air-ground team performance reached a new high.

Several techniques that had been in use for several years were further improved during General Thrash's period of command. One of the most interesting was the insertion and extraction of reconnaissance teams. By their very nature, these teams operated well in advance of friendly lines and in enemy controlled territory. Most of the terrain there was high and forested, and there were few landing zones that permitted helos to land. Teams frequently used long ropes and rappelled in.

Getting out was something else. If it was an emergency situation due to enemy contact, it was not feasible to use a one-man hoist. So flexible ladders were employed. These were as long as 120 feet, and 6-feet wide. They were dropped from the rear ramp of a CH-46, and the pilot would hover at a height so that 20 or 30 feet would lie on the ground. The recon team would hook-on individually to the ladder and the pilot would then execute a vertical climb-out. The team would ride back to base hanging on the end of the ladder, 80 to 100 feet below the chopper and 1,500 to 2,000 feet or more above the ground.

During the extraction, a TAC(A) in an OV-10A would coordinate the air effort. Helo gunships would be directed to provide close-in fires to protect the reconnaissance team on the ground. A-4s and F-4s were available with larger ordnance if more authoritative action was required.

As soon as the CH-46 pilot cleared the pick-up zone, he would turn away from a planned artillery-landing zone line and call in artillery fire to the zone he had just left. This technique became well known to the enemy, so they did not always come too close. If they did not close, the Cobra gunships would work them over while the actual extraction was in process.

Another operation that was continually improved upon as the war progressed was the Sparrow Hawk or Kingfisher, or, as it later became known, the Pacifier. In any case, the basic idea was the same: find the enemy and preempt his move. A package of aircraft was married up to a rifle platoon: CH-46s to provide troop lift, gunships for close-in support, an OV-10A for visual reconnaissance, and a UH-1E for observation and command and control. The OV-10A and gunships would scout out the target area and attempt to find the enemy, and then the CH-46s would insert the reaction force to cordon off the area and fix the enemy. If heavier air support was needed, the command and control helo could request a scramble. This technique proved to be very profitable, and it was often used to seek out the enemy in areas which fired at Marine aircraft, particularly helicopters. Prompt retaliatory action was one of the best measures to reduce this enemy harassment.

Phase Down

The first Marine aviation unit to come into Vietnam after "Shufly" was a LAAM Battalion. The first aviation unit to redeploy without replacement was also a LAAM Battalion. The 2d LAAM Battalion departed in

October 1968 for Twenty-nine Palms, California. The 1st LAAM Battalion followed in August 1969. Even though they had never fired a missile at an enemy aircraft, they had served their purpose.

On 8 June 1969, the President announced his intention to withdraw 25,000 U.S. Servicemen from Vietnam. This increment became known as Keystone Eagle. One HMM departed from the 1stMAW for Futema, Okinawa, and one VMFA departed for Iwakuni, Japan. The 1st LAAM Battalion was part of this increment.

Three months later, on 17 September, another incremental withdrawal was announced, this time 40,500 men from all of the Services—nickname, Keystone Cardinal. The 3dMarDiv was the major unit to leave Vietnam in this increment, and it went to Okinawa. This division plus the 1stMAW (Rear) with headquarters at Iwakuni constituted I MAF. It is to be noted that the 1stMAW (Rear) was not associated organizationally in any way with the 1stMAW in Vietnam. It was simply a temporary title conferred on those aviation units outside of Vietnam that were deployed in WestPac as a component of the Seventh Fleet.

MAG-36 was the largest aviation unit to accompany the division. It deployed to Futema and became the parent group for all Marine helicopter squadrons in 1stMAW (Rear). One HMH, one HMM, and one VMO went to Futema as part of MAG-36. Another HMM returned to Santa Ana, California, to become part of the 3dMAW. One VMA(AW) with 12 A-6 aircraft deployed to Iwakuni and was attached to MAG-15 located there. These moves were all completed by Christmas 1969.

The President announced, on 16 December 1969, his intention to withdraw another 50,000 men. This increment was called Keystone Bluejay. MAG-12 from Chu Lai was the major Marine air unit to leave in this increment. It went to Iwakuni and joined the 1stMAW (Rear). One VMA accompanied it. Another VMA and one VMFA redeployed to El Toro, California, home station of the 3dMAW. One HMH also went to the 3dMAW. It was then stationed at Santa Ana. Keystone Bluejay ended on 15 April.

Before completing Keystone Bluejay, III MAF underwent a change in organization. Lieutenant General Herman Nickerson, Jr., turned over command, on 9 March 1970, to Lieutenant General Keith B. McCutcheon. At the same time General Nickerson was relieved as the senior U.S. Commander in ICTZ by Lieutenant General Melvin Zais, U.S. Army, Commanding General of XXIV Corps. After nearly five years, III MAF relinquished its position as the senior U.S. command in the area. The XXIV Corps headquarters took possession of Camp Horn, on Tien Sha Peninsula across from the city of Da Nang, and III MAF established a new command post at Camp Haskins on Red Beach, very close to where the 3d Battalion, 9th Marines, had come ashore on 8 March five years earlier. Camp Haskins was a Seabee cantonment, where the 32nd Naval Construction Regiment was headquartered.

On 20 April 1970, the President announced the largest withdrawal yet, with 150,000 to leave by 1 May 1971. On 3 June it was announced that 50,000 of these would be out by 15 October 1970. Keystone Robin was the nickname for this undertaking.

Another MAG was included in this increment. MAG-13, along with one VMFA and one VMA(AW), deployed to El Toro. Another VMFA deployed to MCAS Kaneohe, Hawaii, and joined MAG-24 stationed there. These three jet squadrons flew across the Pacific refueling from KC-130s and following the general route, Cubi Point in the Philippines, Guam, Wake, Midway, Kaneohe, and finally El Toro. Jet squadrons in previous increments had followed the same route.

The departure of MAG-13 marked the end of an era at Chu Lai. The last Marine jet flew off the concrete west runway on 11 September and headed east. The air base at Chu Lai was taken over by the U.S. Army's Americal Division.

VMCJ-1 also departed Vietnam and returned to Iwakuni, where it had been stationed prior to its arrival in Vietnam in 1965.

The other major aviation units included in this package were one HMM, which departed for Santa Ana, and Marine Wing Support Group 17, which was relocated at Iwakuni.

The deployments of units in these four increments reduced the 1stMAW from a wing of six aircraft groups and three supporting groups to a wing of two aircraft groups and two supporting groups. The number of aircraft squadrons was now 10, compared to a peak of 26 in 1968 and 1969.

Shortly after the initiation of Keystone Robin, on 1 July 1970, Major General Thrash stepped down as CG of 1stMAW, and Major General Alan J. Armstrong took command. It was to be his lot to continue the reduction of Marine aviation units in Vietnam and probably take the 1stMAW headquarters out of that country.

Retrospect

Marine Corps aviation was in Vietnam in strength for over five years. It was ready when the order was issued to go. The years since Korea had been used to good advantage. New techniques and new equipments were operational. The overall performance from 1965 to 1970 was outstanding.

It was a dynamic period. The Marines deployed to Vietnam in 1965 with UH-34, UH-1, and CH-37 helicopters; A-4, F-B, F-4B, RF-8, and EF-10B jets; and O-1, C-117, and KC-130 propeller aircraft. They added the CH-46, CH-53, AH-1G, A-6, F-9, TA-4F, F-4J, RF-4B, EA-6A, OV-10A, UH-2B, and C-1A. From 1966 on they stopped using the UH-34, CH-47, F-B, F-9, RF-8, EF-10B, and O-1. Only the UH-1, A-4, F-4B, C-117, and KC-130 participated in operations from beginning to end.

Dynamism is one characteristic of a strong and viable air arm. Technical advances continually present the planners with decision points. Marine and Navy planners had done well in the fifties, and that is one reason why so many new aircraft were under development in time to enter the Vietnam War. It is also interesting to note that A-1, A-4, A-7, F-4, F-8, and OV-10A aircraft in use by other Services, U.S. and foreign, were the products of the naval aeronautical organization, as were such air weapons as Sidewinder, Sparrow, Shrike, Snakeye, Bullpup, and Walleye.

The Marine Corps takes pride in the fact that it has always put a great deal of emphasis on planning and looking ahead. Before World

War II, it pioneered the fundamentals of close air support, and during that war it perfected the techniques that are still basic. After that war it entered into the evaluation and application of helicopters to ground combat. When the Korean War began, it was ready to test the concept in a combat environment. Following Korea, it accelerated the development of its concept of a short airfield for tactical support. All three of these major contributions to the state-of-the-art in tactical air warfare were used in Vietnam, not just by the Marines, but by the other Services too. There were other Marine Corps contributions which included the MTDS, TPQ-10, RABFAC beacon, and tactical electronic warfare.

Even while the war in Vietnam was being fought, the Marines were still looking ahead to the future. As was discussed, earlier, the lack of suitable air bases in Vietnam was one major constraint on the buildup of tactical airpower. There are still only two airfields capable of handling jets in ICTZ, and there is still not one south of Saigon. But there are airfields capable of taking light aircraft, KC-130, and Caribou transports and helicopters. And many of these fields could take the Harrier.

The Harrier is a jet vertical take-off and landing strike aircraft developed in England with the help of U.S. dollars, and it is operational now in the Royal Air Force. The Marine Corps saw in the Harrier an aircraft of great potential and initiated procurement action in the FY69 budget for twelve of them. It gave up some F-4 aircraft to get them, and they are coming aboard now. By the end of FY71, the Marines will have their first squadron.

The Harrier will not only permit operations from more sites; it will improve response time in close air support by reducing the time taken to request support (there will be fewer centers and echelons of command to go through), and it can be staged closer to the action, thus cutting flight time. The fact that it can operate from more sites should reduce its vulnerability on the ground, and because it can land vertically there should be a reduction in its accident rate (more landing areas available in an emergency).

The year 1965 was one of buildup. Bases had to be obtained and developed, supply pipelines filled, and initial operating difficulties overcome. The sortie rate for jet aircraft gradually climbed to over 1.0, which was the magic figure used by planners to compute sorties. That means one sortie per day per aircraft assigned. In 1966, the rate went well beyond that, and for the entire period the Marines averaged more than 1.0. When the occasion demanded it, they surged to 1.3, 1.4, or even 1.5 for days at a time. The 1st Wing was a consumer-oriented tactical air support command. If the customer had the demand, the wing would supply the sorties.

Twelve of the Corps' total of 27 fighter-attack squadrons were deployed most of the time and 10 or 11 of these were in Vietnam. Fourteen of its 25 helicopter squadrons were deployed—well over fifty per cent. The same airpower was diminished by the following losses in aircraft in all of Southeast Asia in the period starting 25 August 1962 and ending 10 October 1970.

USMC Aircraft Losses in Southeast Asia

Helicopter combat losses 252
Fixed wing combat losses 173
Helicopter operational losses 172
Fixed wing operational losses 81

Marine Corps aviation surged for over five years in order to sustain the maximum possible strength overseas. The units overseas in turn exceeded all planning factors in terms of output and productivity, under less than ideal conditions.

Marine Corps aviation will leave Vietnam with a sense of accomplishment. It performed its mission for nearly six years and carried out every function in the tactical air book. The innovations and developments it had worked on over the years were proven in combat. The new environment created new challenges for men in Marine aviation, and these were met head-on and solved. The war was the longest, and in many ways the most difficult, one in which Marines have had to participate. The restraints and constraints placed upon the use of air power, and the demanding management reports of all aspects of aviation required by higher authority, imposed additional requirements on staffs with no increase in resources, in most cases, to perform the tasks. In spite of these difficulties, Marine aviation performed in an outstanding manner. An analysis of sorties flown compared to assets on hand will prove that no one outflew the United States Marines.

7 "Marine Air Operations in Northern Europe"

Major Robert J. O'Rourke, USMCR

U.S. Naval Institute *Proceedings*
(November 1980): 53–59

THE NORTHERN FLANK OF NATO's Allied Command Europe consists of Norway, Denmark, and the northern German state, Schleswig-Holstein. Defending the area is the mission of the Commander in Chief, Allied Forces Northern Europe (CinCNorth) whose headquarters are near Oslo, Norway. The maritime nature of the region makes it suitable for the possible employment of U.S. Marines in their traditional role as an amphibious force. Indeed, during the past several years, units of the 4th Marine Amphibious Brigade have participated in large-scale multinational NATO exercises as both an assault and a reinforcing force within the northern region.

These exercises have served to improve the coordination with allied military forces, but many problems remain to be overcome in order for the marines to be effectively employed within CinCNorth's area. A large share of these problems involves the aviation element of a marine air-ground task force (MAGTF) that may be employed within the region.

Marine Air Doctrine: The mission of Marine Corps aviation is stated as follows:

"...to participate as the supporting air component of the Fleet Marine Forces in the seizure and defense of advanced naval bases and for the conduct of such land operations as may be essential to the prosecution of a naval campaign. A collateral function of Marine Corps aviation is to participate as an integral component of naval aviation in the execution of such other Navy functions as the fleet commanders may direct."

In fulfilling this mission, marine air units have, in practice, been employed as the aviation combat element of a MAGTF or, separately but not frequently, as part of a carrier air wing. Their role under the full command of the MAGTF commander receives the majority of emphasis, because it enables the integration of marine air and ground operations to a high degree; this tactical integration is a distinguishing feature of U.S. Marine doctrine.

In order to achieve the required degree of integration with ground operations, marine air operations are commanded at the highest level within a MAGTF. Command and control are exercised through the highly sophisticated marine air command and control system (MACCS). This system is designed to function during an amphibious operation and subsequent land operations. The system is ideal when the MAGTF is assigned a large geographical area in which to operate. Within a large area, the MAGTF commander is usually responsible for controlling and defending the associated airspace sector. The command and control system is capable of performing all of the functions required for airspace control as well as control of air defense forces within its assigned sector. The MACCS is also capable of coordinating these functions with adjacent sector air command and control systems.

This arrangement becomes a problem, however, during operations in which a sector of airspace cannot be reserved for exclusive MAGTF use. Such circumstances are likely in Northern Europe. There is a clear danger that autonomous operations of Marine Corps aviation could cause interference with operations of allied air forces, which are commanded and controlled through their own organizational structures. Avoiding mutual interference in this case would require that the MAGTF commander coordinate his air operations with those of the local allied air commander, who is also the authority responsible for providing local airspace control.

A number of questions spring immediately to mind:

- How are conflicting requirements for the use of common airspace to be resolved?
- How do Marine Corps fighter-interceptor aircraft and Hawk surface-to-air missiles perform the air defense of the MAGTF within airspace that is already defended by, let us say, German fighter planes and Hawk missiles?
- Who should decide that an enemy interdiction target is properly the mission of the local allied air force or the MAGTF air element?

It is not enough to say that these items should be treated on a case-by-case basis, or that they will be "coordinated." Sound military planning requires that the framework for resolving these problems be established prior to conflict, or at least prior to the commitment of forces. Experience during live and synthetic exercises in which elements of the Marine Corps have been employed in Northern Europe as a reinforcement force has shown that this framework is not easily constructed.

Relative Force Strengths: Aside from the obvious technical complexity involved in resolving these issues, there are a number of other aspects, including the size and capability of a MAGTF air element in relation to allied air forces. The Norwegian Air Force consists of 115 combat aircraft and 42 helicopters. There is one surface-to-air missile battalion armed with Nike Hercules missiles. Scheduled for future procurement are 72 F-16

Fighters, one Sea King helicopter, and 40 "Roland II" mobile surface-to-air missiles. In the Danish Air Force are 114 combat aircraft and 12 SAM squadrons. Eight of the latter are armed with Nike Hercules missiles and four with "improved Hawks." The Danes have 58 F-I6A/B fighters on order.

The air picture in the Baltic Approaches area is improved considerably by the German Naval Air Arm and units of the German Air Force that are stationed in Schleswig-Holstein. Charged with a primarily anti-shipping role, the German Naval Air Arm possesses approximately 130 tactical aircraft, 21 "Sea King" helicopters, and 30 utility aircraft. The 85 F-104 aircraft will be replaced by the Panavia Tornado giving the force a very credible all-weather attack capability in the Baltic. Two squadrons of G-91 aircraft of the German Air Force will be replaced by the "Alpha Jet," thereby maintaining a respectable close air support capability for ground forces in the Schleswig-Holstein area, and two squadrons of RF-4E aircraft provide quite satisfactory tactical air reconnaissance capability.

During a period of tension or war, reinforcement squadrons of the U.S., United Kingdom, and Canadian Air Forces would presumably deploy quickly to pre-planned North European Command air bases in all three subordinate command areas. While these reinforcement forces would add significantly to the tactical air assets available to CinCNorth, they are considered by many to be insufficient to make up the balance of what is needed in the area. It is worth noting that Norway and Denmark do not permit foreign forces to be permanently stationed on their home territory during peacetime.

As for the Marine Corps, the aviation combat element of a MAGTF is task-organized to fulfill its role in accomplishing assigned missions. If the MAGTF is the size of a marine amphibious force (MAF) it may include an entire marine air wing with over 200 fixed-wing aircraft and more than 170 helicopters. Added to this would be a Hawk battalion, Redeye surface-to-air missiles, and a complete air command and control system.

The variety and sophistication of a marine air wing that could deploy to Northern Europe are illustrated by the following:

Type	Function	Number
EA-6	Electronic Warfare	6
RF-4	Air Reconnaissance	6
A-6E	All-Weather Attack/Strike	36
F-4J	Attack and All-Weather Intercept	60
A-4M	Attack/Strike	32
AV-8A	Attack	40
OV-10A	Observation/Forward Air Control	12
CH-46	Medium Lift (Helicopter)	72
CH-53	Heavy Lift (Helicopter)	42
UH-1	Utility Lift (Helicopter)	42
AH-1	Close-in Fire Support (Helicopter)	18
KC-130	Aerial Refueling/Assault Support	12

The employment of the aviation combat element of a MAF-size force within any one of these subordinate Northern European Command areas would be a major infusion of tactical air power. In some cases, it may not be possible to employ so large an air force, because the base facilities to do so may be nonexistent. Although a marine amphibious brigade (MAB)–size force is significantly smaller than a MAF, it may contain more than 65 fixed-wing aircraft and almost 100 helicopters. With a MAB-size force only the depth of the problem is lessened. In either case, the size and capability of MAGTF aviation is significant enough to merit the interest and concern of any air commander in whose airspace and on whose ramp space it operates.

Conflicting Doctrines? Air commanders in Northern Europe adhere to the principles of NATO tactical air doctrine. This doctrine requires centralized command and control of air forces at the highest practicable levels. Air commanders direct the total air effort within their areas by exercising operational control of their assigned or attached tactical air forces. The problem with Marine Corps aircraft operating within their areas is that it is neither assigned nor attached to these NATO air commanders.

Many NATO commanders and staff officers, therefore, are convinced that in order to resolve the conflicts that will arise between in-place air forces and MAGTF air assets most quickly and efficiently, Marine Corps aircraft must also be included under the operational control of the local air commander, rather than remaining under the operational control of its marine commander. This solution is probably the simplest and would clearly enable the local air commander to apply the principles of concentration of force, economy and unity of effort, all of which are established NATO tactical air principles.

To the marines, however, this solution is no solution at all. Placing its air element under the operational control of a local air commander in practical terms means breaking up the air-ground team concept of the MAGTF organization. This restructuring would hurt the combat capability of Marine Corps ground forces who would not be able to count on their own air power being made available when and where it was desired. The marines are concerned that once their air assets are under the operational control of other than a Marine Corps commander, they may be used primarily for missions other than support of the marine ground force. The potential contribution of MAGTF air to the size and capability of Northern European Command air forces would indicate that this concern is not without foundation.

Defending the MAGTF concept extends beyond good tactical thinking. Marine aircraft are purchased by American taxpayers, maintained by marine mechanics, and flown by marine pilots in order to fulfill the mission of marine aviation. Marine aviation is oriented toward support of an essentially naval campaign, and its training emphasizes a close relationship with its ground forces. NATO air forces are oriented toward an air campaign against the enemy; they are not organized or trained to work as closely with ground forces. Close air support, for example, is a priority mission of Marine Corps attack aircraft but is not accorded high priority by NATO air commanders. To place marine air power under the operational control of other than a Marine Corps commander is to strip it of its distinguishing characteristic and make it appear to be no different than any other air force. This would also make the ground combat element indistinguishable from comparable army formations, except that the marines might be more lightly equipped. Many marines think that this could be used by budget cutters and critics of the Marine Corps to reduce its size and capability by arguing that its function could be performed more economically by the U.S. Air Force and the U.S. Army.

Marines defend their tactical air arm and the air- ground team concept with religious intensity, and they balk at any suggestion that marine aircrews and aircraft be used to fill deficiencies in the air forces of NATO allies. This is not to say that the marines are unwilling to provide air support to local air commanders in whose areas they may be operating. On the contrary, they have demonstrated their willingness to do so during exercises within Northern European Command, but in each case the air support was provided only after the MAGTF commander had satisfied his own needs first. While this procedure has been accepted by most officers within NATO circles, it has been done with reluctance by many because it does not give the local air commanders the degree of control within their areas that they think is required. On the other hand, there are a number of NATO stall officers who, privately, do not accept this arrangement at all and fail to see any compatibility between NATO and Marine Corps tactical air doctrines. Neither of these attitudes reflects the enthusiasm toward marine aviation that might be expected for a force with its combat potential. Another factor which further dampens enthusiasm is the belief by many NATO officers that marine aviation will not arrive anyway within the region in sufficient time to make any contribution to the total air effort, even under this arrangement.

In my view, the attitude of those NATO staff officers toward Marine Corps aviation is unfortunate. In fairness to them, however, this attitude is understandable, given the conservative and often doctrinaire manner in which marine commanders and staff officers have presented their case. Despite these attitudes, however, considerable progress has been made toward achieving a workable solution, because the parties to the issue agree that a solution must be found and that the general guidelines for possible marine air operations within the Northern European Command must be established during peacetime.

Any solution that is obtained must establish a relationship of coordination and mutual support between Marine Corps aviation and the air forces of the local air commander, and it must recognize the genuine tactical requirements of each force. In practical terms, this means that NATO commanders must accept the MAGTF concept and the command and control authority of the MAGTF commander over his organic air assets. This also means that the operations of the marine aviation element must be coordinated and frequently even integrated with those of local air commanders, who must be authorized to exercise at least a coordinating authority over certain MAGTF air operations. The need for coordination should be obvious if effective control of airspace is to be exercised by the local air commander. The need for varying degrees of integration of such area-oriented operations as air defense (both fighter and SAM), interdiction, electronic warfare, tactical air reconnaissance, and air control should also be apparent, so that these operations are conducted in the most militarily efficient manner. This can be done without compromising the virtues of the Marine Corps air-ground team.

The solution to the problem of marine air operations within the region is no further away than convincing NATO and Marine Corps authorities that their interests, forces, and air doctrines, in fact, are compatible. Plans that reflect this compatibility must be drafted and approved; ultimately they must be tested during live exercises. In this manner, the relationship between U.S. Marine aviation and allied air forces in the Northern European Command in a reinforcement scenario will be codified and considerable air power of these wings will probably not be available to the Northern European Command during periods of tension and the initial stages of hostilities. Other air organizations within the area are integrated at the level of the principal subordinate commander, who, because of national basing policies, has infrequent opportunity to exercise operational control over a large number of aircraft with varied and sophisticated capabilities. Reinforcement air units to the Northern European Command will arrive as individual squadrons with individual capabilities. Therefore, time will be required before the air organization of Northern European Command air commanders will be able to function at the desired level of efficiency and effectiveness.

Other Missions: Implementing the above ideas would remove the major obstacle to smooth marine air operations within the northern flank. Under the present MAGTF concept of employing marine assets, this would appear to be sufficient. But, employing a balanced or traditionally configured MAGTF in a reinforcing role seems to be a misuse of such a MAGTF, which is more suitable for autonomous amphibious operations. The problems associated with employing such a MAGTF as a reinforcement force suggest to this author that, if purely land reinforcements are desired, NATO should ask for army formations; air force planes should be requested for air reinforcements. This is not to say that the MAGTF concept is inflexible; in fact, the flexibility of a MAGTF structure makes it an ideal reinforcement force for this region, and, as mentioned earlier, there are also collateral missions of marine air that do not involve the MAGTF concept at all. Restructuring a MAGTF, or using Marine Corps air separately, in this region may possess advantages that are worthwhile to discuss, even though such use is contrary to current concepts for U.S. Marine Corps employment within the region.

Under the category of collateral missions conducted in support of the fleet, a task-organized aviation element of air group or reduced air wing size could be profitably employed in North Norway or the Baltic Approaches. The purpose of employing marine air elements in these locations would be to bolster the allied defenses of the sea exits by projecting fleet offensive air power from land bases into Warsaw Pact territory, while simultaneously improving local allied air defenses. A Marine Corps air group could be quickly deployed from the United States during a period of increasing political tension, and its varied and sophisticated capabilities would provide an immediate indication of U.S. loyalty to its NATO commitment.

An appealing feature of such an air group is its task organization; it arrives as a complete package with all of the capabilities to conduct modern air warfare. Capabilities include close and deep offensive air support, air defense (fighter and SAM), tactical air reconnaissance, electronic warfare, assault support (troop lift, cargo transport, aerial refueling, close-in force support), and air command and control.

The tactical value of task-organized Marine Corps air groups to either North Norway or the Baltic Approaches, or possibly even both, is the major argument for this concept. Recent news releases in Norway report the inadequate air defenses within the area, particularly at airfields that may be vital reception facilities for external reinforcements. These air fields would undoubtedly be subjected to heavy air attack during the initial stages of a conflict with the nations of the Warsaw Pact. A Marine Corps air group that possesses both fighter/interceptor aircraft (F-4s and later F-18s) as well as Hawk and Redeye surface-to-air missiles would be able to provide strong air defense of vital airheads. A-6 Intruders and A-4 Skyhawks with electronic warfare support from EA-6B Prowlers, reconnaissance support from RF-4s, fighter support from F-4s, and in-flight refueling support from KC-130s would be able to carry the air battle to Warsaw Pact territory and/or forces, thereby relieving some of the pressure on allied forces and territory. In addition to the obvious direct benefits that would be enjoyed by Northern European command allied forces as a result of such Marine Corps air operations, naval commanders of Supreme Allied Command Atlantic would be a major beneficiary. Marine offensive air operations would threaten Warsaw Pact naval forces attempting to enter the Norwegian Sea or breach the belts formed by the Danish Islands. These same aircraft would be capable of conducting offensive counter air operations against Soviet air bases in the Kola Peninsula or eastern Europe in order to reduce the threat of Soviet anti-ship missile-armed air forces.

This concept can be applied more realistically perhaps by employing a properly structured marine air-ground task force. It would be organized primarily to conduct an air-oriented rather than a land-oriented naval campaign. The ground element of such a MAGTF would be employed as a security force for air bases, while the air element conducts operations that directly support allied commanders both on land and at sea.

This arrangement might be ideal for an exposed area such as North Norway, whose air bases should be considered priority objectives for Soviet airborne and/or amphibious assault. A secure airhead in North Norway, in the view of this author, is not a reasonable military assumption under present arrangements. The concept of forward-deployed, land-based naval air in the form of an air-heavy MAGTF makes such an assumption possible. This view is generally shared by Commander Bruce Van Heertum, USN, whose excellent article on a similar subject appeared in the September 1979 issue of the *Marine Corps Gazette*. Van Heertum points out the limited number of aircraft carriers that are available for the projection of naval air power and argues for the use of land-based Marine Corps planes to supplement the carrier-based aircraft. He concludes that such use of marine air would free the aircraft carriers to concentrate on open-ocean duties. I would add that, in the case of operations in the Norwegian Sea, proper forward basing of marine aircraft would permit the Strategic Allied Commander Atlantic to hold his carriers in relatively secure reserve on the southern and less threatening side of the Greenland–Iceland–United Kingdom Gap, where they could provide needed security for air and sea reinforcements to Europe. If land-based marine aircraft were to succeed in greatly reducing the capabilities of the Soviet Northern Fleet by attacking from bases in North Norway, the use of carriers in the Norwegian Sea may not be necessary, and the ships could be profitably employed elsewhere. If Marine Corps aircraft were only partially successful against the Soviet power in Kola, carriers could then be employed in the Norwegian Sea at reduced risk.

These concepts are not without problems, however. Present basing facilities may not be adequate for bedding down a large force of aircraft. Furthermore, dedicated air and sealift for rapid deployment may also not be available, at least within the constraints of present plans. Pre-stocking equipment and munitions in order to improve deployment time and reduce lift requirements is an expensive and politically difficult solution to this problem. But these problems are not insurmountable if NATO and national authorities determine that such deployment of Marine Corps aircraft offers advantages over present piecemeal reinforcement concepts.

Conclusion: The employment of marine aviation, supported as necessary by ground forces, as a landward extension of carrier aviation is a realistic and tactically advantageous method of using Marine Corps reinforcements to the Northern European Command. Such employment can be accomplished within the marine air-ground task force concept, although the MAGTF would be decidedly air oriented and be assigned almost exclusively air missions. In this light, reinforcement by a ground-oriented MAGTF that is assigned primarily missions involving a land campaign is seen as offering fewer advantages. This is the prevailing concept of U.S. Marine reinforcement to the region, however. Under this prevailing concept, the amphibious capability of a traditional MAGTF is quickly lost, and it, in fact, becomes nothing more than another ground unit with its own troublesome, but powerful, air arm. A traditionally configured MAGTF should be employed in its traditional role, amphibious assault, and not squandered as just another infantry force. There will certainly be missions enough for such a force in any future conflict, and amphibious assault should still be considered the cornerstone of Marine Corps operations. But the flexibility of marine forces and doctrine enables the Marine Corps to be employed in roles other than amphibious assault to great advantage. In order to be so employed, a larger and more independent role for marine aviation is necessary, and, given this role, the Marine Corps will make a contribution to this region of NATO that can be made by no other force.

A 1967 graduate of the Naval Academy, **Major O'Rourke** was a 1971 Olmsted Scholar to the University of Heidelberg and received an M.A. in international relations from Boston University in 1973. He has had combat experience as an infantry officer and has served as an A-4 pilot, instructor pilot, and tactics instructor. From 1978 to 1980, he was a staff officer in air operations at Headquarters, Allied Forces Northern Europe in Norway. He is now attending the Harvard University Graduate School of Business and serving in Marine Corps Reserve Squadron VMA-322 at South Weymouth, Massachusetts.

8 "Stop Quibbling and Win the War"

Major John E. Valliere, USAF

U.S. Naval Institute *Proceedings*
(December 1990): 38–43

The fundamental concept of employment of [Marine aviation] will remain "centralized command and coordination," and "decentralized control and execution."

> —Fleet Marine Force Reference Publication 14-5 Marine
> Air Command and Control System Operational Concept[1]

The most effective means for directing and executing an air effort is centralized control and decentralized execution.

> –Air Force Manual 1-1, U.S. Air Force Basic Doctrine

Relatively few interservice command and control problems arise when U.S. Marine Corps aircraft are involved in amphibious operations. But they begin to surface when Marine Corps and Air Force aircraft support sustained operations ashore.

WHEN I ARRIVED at the Marine Corps Command and Staff College, I had only a vague idea of what a Marine Air-Ground Task Force (MAGTF) was. Like many Air Force officers, I had little idea of a MAGTF's strengths or weaknesses. I had never heard of an "Omnibus Agreement for Command and Control of USMC [U.S. Marine Corps] Tactical Airpower." I quickly learned that my Marine Corps contemporaries knew all about the Omnibus Agreement—and that I was, by virtue of my blue suit, in the enemy camp. To them, it was obvious the Air Force wanted to steal their airplanes.

I listened to the arguments and became familiar with what I call the "Battle of the Letters."[2] (See "The Air Force Letter," and "The Marine Corps Letter," accompanying this article; both have been condensed.) I soon realized that Marines were teaching each other my doctrine and the Air Force was trying to teach itself Marine Corps doctrine. I reached one more seemingly obvious and irrefutable conclusion: A commander should—and will—use all his assets to accomplish his mission.

During peacetime, however, the services have occupied their time with a semantic argument concerning the joint control of airpower. The Marine Corps and the Air Force have been on opposite sides of the argument—with the Navy generally taking the Marine Corps' position. It all centers on the 1986 Joint Chiefs of Staff (JCS) Omnibus Agreement, a single paragraph that states the MAGTF commander retains operational control of his organic Marine air assets. It also authorizes the joint force commander to assign missions to Marine air "to ensure unity of effort in accomplishment of his overall mission." The Omnibus Agreement came out of the JCS tank during deliberations on joint counterair doctrine, which uses terminology that brings into play the semantic problems.

JCS Publication 3-01.1, the resulting joint doctrine, says that a joint force commander will "normally" establish a "joint force air component commander (JFACC)." The JFACC, by definition, can exercise operational control of air assets. Those words "operational control," conflict with the Omnibus Agreement, which says the MAGTF commander retains operational control of his forces. In many scenarios, the JFACC would be an Air Force officer. Since Marines argue—correctly, in my opinion— that the MAGTF's air assets cannot be detached to function directly under the JFACC, does it follow that the JFACC must assume operational control of the whole MAGTF in order to gain access to its air assets? Marine Corps ground combat officers rightfully resist being commanded by the Air Force.

In fact, a JFACC need not exercise operational control of air assets. The JCS definition of the term places such a command function in the hands of the joint force commander. The JFACC's role centers on "... planning, coordination, allocation, and tasking . . . [to] . . . ensure unity of effort in the accomplishment of the [joint force commander's] overall mission." A JFACC does not need operational control or command of a MAGTF to accomplish that. The Air Force was quite clear on that point in its contribution to the Battle of the Letters, with the statement, "A JFACC does not require Operational Control of air forces to complete assigned tasks."

As to the service affiliation of the JFACC, often the source of consternation for Marines and the Navy, the Air Force does not expect the JFACC to be an Air Force officer in all cases. A spokesman for the Air Force's doctrine office at the Pentagon stated emphatically that the Air Force expects the JFACC to represent the "owner" of the preponderance of air forces. One can extrapolate this to mean the owner of the most tactical air assets would be the JFACC; airlift, airborne warning and control, and special mission aircraft might likely be discounted.

While the Air Force does not insist on command or operational control of all air assets for a JFACC, it does insist a JFACC should be precisely what the JCS stated—a normal member of a joint command. This is a direct result of the Air Force's experience. During operations in North Africa in World War II, air assets were piecemealed out to the front. This failure to concentrate airpower cost lives and missions. Leaders up to and including General Eisenhower, came to believe in what the Air Force refers to today as "centralized control with decentralized execution." As the quotes at the beginning of this article indicate, this is no different from the doctrine of the U.S. Marine Corps. The Marines insist on centralized allocation of airpower within the MAGTF's aviation combat element, yet seem to argue against it when the MAGTF is integrated into a joint operation.

Joint commands are in essence large MAGTFs. They have air, naval, and land components whose purpose is to accomplish the mission set forth by the strategic authorities. The synergism existing within the MAGTF must also be possessed by a joint command. The concepts of command and control existing within a MAGTF that create this synergism must also be applied to the joint command. Certainly one of these is the centralized supervision and tasking of air missions.

So far I have worn my Air Force hat and supported the JFACC position as seen by the Air Force. What of Marine Corps concerns? The Marine Corps' doctrine stems from its own history of amphibious and expeditionary warfare, a style of combat that has proved vital to the nation repeatedly during this century. It has also refined the nature and the capabilities of the Marine Corps. Lacking the Army's heavy corps artillery, for example, MAGTF's have come to rely on organic airpower to provide fire support. The mobile, expeditionary nature of the Marine Corps suits the service best for short-duration missions, often with limited objectives. When the Marines are operating as part of a larger force, the joint commander would have to make the MAGTF the focus of effort and the MAGTF's air assets would be employed in the support of the MAGTF's mission. During this stage, if airplanes moved from one part of the theater to another, it would likely be Air Force airplanes moving to aid the Marines, not vice versa.

Once Marine operations ashore become sustained operations, which happened in the Vietnam War, the expeditionary doctrine does not apply as directly. The MAGTF will not be the focus of effort all the time. The Omnibus Agreement, according to the original JCS message, was directed specifically to "sustained operations ashore," when Marine air missions may well be needed some place else. Until that point, however, the Marines have every right to get the full air support they brought with them, and more. The United States has a Marine Corps for its self-contained expeditionary capability; nothing should be done to compromise that capability. Further, everything should be done to try to employ the Marines in expeditionary missions. Sustained operations ashore should be an exception, not a rule. Such missions are better suited for the Air Force and the Army.

The Omnibus Agreement is in line with both Marine Corps and Air Force doctrine. The joint counterair doctrine tasks the MAGTF to provide only certain sorties to the joint task force, and these sorties would be used for priority missions by the joint force commander. What is lacking now is not doctrine but understanding.

How do we get understanding on both sides of the issue? The Goldwater-Nichols Act provides much of the answer. Its demands for truly joint professional military education should lead to mutual understanding and cooperation in time. Air Force officers must come to understand the unique capabilities of the amphibious, expeditionary Marines. Marine Corps officers must learn that Air Force doctrine really is not different from their own.

Concerns on both sides of the JFACC issue are well-founded; unfortunately, gaining understanding through education will come slowly. Personalities play a role. Some high-ranking individuals will always have ideas not completely in accord with their own service's doctrine. Certainly some Air Force generals will always think they should be the JFACC, even though the Air Force does not feel this way. Some will say that an Air Force officer should be JFACC when they mean that a flier should fill the role. Joint education should teach officers to avoid semantic pitfalls. Particularly important to avoid are the problems caused by explaining someone else's doctrine. In the Battle of the Letters, the Air Force has misrepresented Marine Corps doctrine and the Marines have returned the favor.

Education is needed if we are to overcome long-held views, such as the following, a response to an earlier version of this article from a retired

Marine Corps officer: "The Marine Corps believes in balanced combined arms teams. Unlike other services it is organized, equipped, and trained on the basis of this concept. It will deploy and fight on this basis, and its commanders will insist on unity of command and unity of their balanced teams because these are essential to combat effectiveness. This is not a difficult concept to grasp; there are no semantical hurdles except those introduced by others with parochial interests to serve."[3]

Knowledge gained in the classroom cannot remain there or parochialism will never die. Officers who have had the benefit of attending other service schools must serve as missionaries to those who have not had the experience. Those who are sent from joint schools to joint staffs must endeavor to learn even more about the doctrine and abilities of sister services and take that knowledge forward. This is the reason behind the Goldwater-Nichols Act that requires previous joint duty of those officers promoted to the flag and general ranks.

No one ever seems surprised or concerned that a joint force commander has the authority to use his assets to accomplish his mission. If the United States is committed to combat, it must win. On the days when the bullets are not flying, we should resist the temptation to engage in semantic arguments and instead concentrate on learning how to give a joint commander the means to win.

The Air Force Letter

Recent Navy and Marine Corps actions at the Service level seem to indicate the existence of an organized effort to limit the use of the Joint Force Air Component Commander (JFACC) in joint doctrine and in OPLANs/CONPLANs [operational plans/contingency plans]. This letter contains basic JFACC information which can be used by personnel working contingency operations, war planning, command relationships, doctrine, and exercises and is provided to permit the Air Force to speak with one voice on this issue.

... This paper provides proposed counter arguments to those used by the Navy and Marine Corps to limit or eliminate use of "Air Component Commander" or "Joint Force Air Component Commander" (JFACC) in OPLANS/ CONPLANS and joint doctrine.

Argument: The term "Air Component Commander (ACC)" cannot be used when the CINC [commander-in-chief] elects to use a Service Component command organizational structure; change ACC to "Air Force Component Commander."

Response: (a) The term ACC is not defined in JCS Pub 1. The Navy/Marines see the term as meaning a fully functional command organization; the Air Force contends that the terms ACC and JFACC are synonymous ... The Joint Chiefs of Staff reaffirmed and inserted the "Omnibus Agreement" in JCS Pub 26 and verbally agreed that the terms "ACC" in the Omnibus Agreement and "JFACC" in Pub 26 were identical in meaning ... (b) JCS Pub 2 allows the CINC to organize his command essentially any way he wants ...

Argument: A Joint Force Air Component Commander is limited to conducting counterair operations by JCS Pub 26.

Response: (a) The definition of JFACC in JCS Pub 26 and Pub 1 does not restrict the use of a JFACC. Pub 26 talks about using a JFACC for counterair operations because Pub 26 is Joint Doctrine for Counterair Operations. (b) The 1986 Omnibus Agreement requires the MAGTF commander to provide sorties for air defense, long-range interdiction, long-range reconnaissance, and sorties in excess of MAGTF direct support requirements to the Joint Force Commander for tasking through the Air Component Commander (or JFACC). Omnibus Agreement obviously does not restrict a JFACC to counterair operations ...

Argument: The JFACC can only be designated at the Theater commander level, it cannot be used in unified commands, or Joint Task Forces.

Response: The "Scope" paragraph in chapter 1 of JCS Pub 26 provides clear guidance: "The joint doctrine established . . . applies to unified commands and their subordinate commands and those joint task forces that may be established by the President, Secretary of Defense, or commander of a unified command for the conduct of specific operations." . . . The Navy and Marine Corps arguments do not hold water. JFACC is the only JCS approved tool for a joint force commander to task, coordinate, and unify the efforts of all of the air forces available for his assigned mission.

. . . General P. X. Kelley, U.S. Marine Corps [then Commandant of the Marine Corps] in White Letter No. 4-86 dated 18 March 1986, fully endorsed the contents, spirit, and intent of the Chairman, Joint Chief of Staffs message announcing approval of JCS Pub 26, the definition of JFACC, and the 1986 Omnibus Agreement for command and control of USMC TACAIR in sustained operations ashore (above). General Kelley went on to say, "The bottom line is that the Joint Force Commander is in charge. If he *personally* believes that he has higher priority missions for any, repeat any, Marine TACAIR, he has the authority to utilize them as he sees fit." (Emphasis in original.)

. . . Since the Navy and Marine Corps have been trying to keep JFACC duties limited to counterair operations, it is advisable to include words in OPLANs/CONPLANs which do not unduly limit the scope of the JFACC responsibilities . . . the best arguments are well thought out methods showing how a JFACC can assist the joint force commander in completing the mission(s) assigned.

. . . Final comment: If a joint force commander is reluctant to grant the JFACC the scope of responsibilities desired, take what is possible and make the seed grow. A joint force commander will expand the duties and responsibilities of organizations that function effectively and help him achieve the joint force assigned missions.

The Marine Corps Letter

Last May, the Air Force distributed a letter on the subject [of the Joint Force Air Component Commander] to its major commands and key officers in joint assignments. The apparent purpose of the letter was to educate readers on the details of the Joint Force Air Component Commander (JFACC) concept approved by the Joint Chiefs of Staff in 1986.

. . . [My] letter conveys information about and affirms the Marine Corps position of support for the JFACC concept. It also provides a comparison of the differing but operationally compatible Air Force and Marine Corps philosophies of force employment.

The doctrinal framework for employment of a MAGTF is the effective integration of combined arms for combat operations at the tactical level . . . Accordingly, the Marine Corps organizes, equips, trains, and provides to unified commanders for employment forces of combined arms, together with organic supporting air components, called MAGTFs.

The underpinnings of Air Force doctrine support a focus on an overarching air battle with a subset thereof, the provision of close air support to maneuvering land battle formations. Air Force doctrine emphasizes centralized control ". . . under a single air commander who directs the employment of forces at a level of command from which the overall air situation can best be judged." Tactical air assets—of whatever Service component—are held to be national assets to be placed under centralized management.

. . . The basic orientation of the two Services differs notably. For the Air Force, the air battle takes precedence. The consolidation of air assets, functionally, was its justification for independence from the U.S. Army in 1947. The Air Force since its inception has based centralized management at the theater level on operations research showing that management-oriented efficiency (single manager for air) provides better general support.

The Marine Corps considers organic MAGTF aviation as a supporting arm in operations where the ground battle is paramount. Marine aviation is organized, trained, and equipped to be the aviation combat element of a MAGTF that is immediately responsive to the needs of the Marine ground combat element commander. The integrated employment of MAGTF aviation is designed to offset and augment the Marine ground commander's relatively light organic fire support. The directly available, short response time criteria for aviation employment makes it an acceptable alternative to artillery or naval gunfire . . .

. . . [Also] at issue is how the battlefield is developed. Air Force operators and planners tend to view the battlefield "horizontally" on the premise that all aircraft with certain characteristics (e.g., speed, range, and flexibility) or capabilities (e.g., antiair, reconnaissance, interdiction/deep air support) should be under Air Force control. The focus is on interdicting well beyond the fire support coordination line (FSCL) those enemy warfighting components vital to the prosecution of war.

Marine Corps operators and planners see the battlefield "vertically" emphasizing integrated combined arms operations in relationship to the MAGTF area of responsibility (AOR). The MAGTF commander executes a ground scheme of maneuver, with a supporting air plan that includes extensive close air support short of the FSCL . . .

. . . Flowing from the above, the philosophy of joint integration of force for combat differs between the two Services. The Air Force subscribes to a functional organization for battle (air, land, sea) in which tactical, fixed-wing air support is integrated, organizationally, no lower than the joint force level. It holds a philosophy that joint force mission attainment can be best achieved by the application of all fixed-wing, tactical air power—regardless of Service component—by a designated, functionally-oriented, air component commander exercising OPCON over all TACAIR [tactical aviation] assets.

. . . The Marine Corps subscribes to a philosophy of joint operations which focuses on overall joint force mission attainment through employment of Service components consistent with their designed warfighting capabilities and in a manner designed to exploit those capabilities. It supports the integration of force at the joint level through mission planning, coordination, and direction of forces, rather than through consolidated command of subordinate components' organic assets.

Notes

1. Emphasis added. Marines will be quick to note FMFRP 14-5 is not doctrine. The quote is a good summation of Marine aviation doctrine, however. The Air Force Manual covers far more than tactical airpower. To compare doctrines more accurately, see Tactical Air Command Manual 2-1, Tactical Air Operations (15 April 1978 with Change 1 of 14 May 1982) and Fleet Marine Force Manual 5-1, *Marine Aviation* (24 August 1979).

2. The two letters in question are the 5 May 1988 letter to Air Force commanders from Brigadier General Thomas E. Eggers, Air Force Deputy Director of Plans, on the Air Force staff; and the 9 March 1989 letter to Marines from Major General Michael P. Sullivan, Deputy Commander for Warfighting, Marine Corps Combat Development Command.

3. Colonel J. E. Greenwood, U.S. Marine Corps (Retired) letter to the author dated 30 April 1990.

Major Valliere is a student at the Marine Corps School of Advanced Warfighting, Quantico, Virginia. After a tour as an F-111 weapon system officer he graduated from flight training and now flies C-130s.

9 "Who Really Needs Marine TacAir?"

Lieutenant Colonel Thomas Linn, USMC

U.S. Naval Institute *Proceedings*
(October 1992): 40–44

The answer is simple if the nation requires an expeditionary avi-ation capability in the future. The Navy, Air Force, and Army do. Marine tactical aviation—here, Marine F/A-18 Hornets over the Kuwait battlefield last year—provides a versatility not matched by other supporting arms.

SENATOR SAM NUNN (D-GA), Chairman of the Senate Armed Services Committee, recently questioned the rationale underlying "four air forces" within the U.S. armed forces. Echoes of Senator Barry Goldwater (R-AZ)![1]

This fundamental question and others posed by Senator Nunn are relevant to a defense establishment created for a now-ended Cold War. Military capabilities and missions, long taken for granted, warrant reex-amination.

Such a reexamination is particularly relevant in the case of the "fourth" air force: the Marine fixed-wing fighter and attack tactical air-craft (TacAir). In essence, Marine tactical aviation serves as this nation's expeditionary air force, albeit within the framework of a Marine Air Ground Task Force (MAGTF). But whether the country needs "four air forces" is the wrong question. The real question is: Will the nation need an expeditionary air force capability in the future, and, if so, which service should provide it?

The discriminator for each service's air arm is in how it is used to carry out its assigned roles and missions. For the Marine Corps, roles and missions have been the primary consideration for developing capabilities, an approach best characterized by the following extract from the report on the 1952 Marine Corps Act: ". . . its [the Marine Corps'] purpose is to provide a balanced force for a naval campaign and, at the same time, a ground and air striking force ready to suppress or contain international disturbances short of war . . . such a force would better enable the Army and Air Force to concentrate on their major responsibility of preparing for all-out war."[2]

Marine TacAir figures prominently in this mandated force-in-readiness. It makes the Marine Air Ground Task Force the most complete and readily employable force found at the tactical level. As one U.S. Air Force officer wrote, "joint commands are in essence larger MAGTFs."[3] But even this laudatory comparison does not adequately describe the Marine Air Ground Task Force's capabilities. Such a task force with its own tactical aircraft is made-to-order for a battlefield's four dimensions—the most critical dimension being time. This force can be inserted rapidly into an austere environment in response to unforeseen, time-sensitive crises. Such capabilities make Marine Air Ground Task Forces important to planners.

The Marine Corps is unique in its tailored capability to seize bases and establish expeditionary airfields for the introduction of tactical aircraft in a particular theater of operations. Under such conditions, Marine tactical aircraft can contribute to local air superiority until the Air Force establishes itself. Inclusive in this expeditionary capability is the ability to establish the Marine Corps Air Command and Control System—which is presently the only means of interoperability between the respective Air Force and Navy systems. Also, the existence of integrated air-ground operations within the Marine Expeditionary Force (MEF) buys time for the Army and Air Force to work out the complexities of air-land battle. These capabilities are not only another aspect of the Marine Corps' "insurance policy" in the event of austere conditions, but are also the critical link in the transition from sea power to the requisite air and land power for a continental campaign.

What makes a Marine task force rapidly employable is the ongoing unity of effort between its air and ground forces. All elements of the task force—from tactical aircraft to combat service support units—subscribe to the same doctrine, possess interoperable equipment, and routinely train together. In addition, the Marine Air Command and Control System is integrated with the ground combat element's fire support coordination effort to ensure air and ground weapons fully complement each other.

Such a unity of effort is not easily achieved, nor is its importance widely recognized. The integration of air-ground operations is complex and time-consuming. As Allan R. Millet and I. B. Holley wrote in *Case Studies in the Development of Close Air Support,* an air-ground evolution of such complexity as close air support requires established procedures and considerable practice.[4] But, as these and other contributors to the study have noted, such procedures have resulted in discord and friction between the services, largely because of differences in doctrine. Only after a considerable period have operating procedures between air and ground forces been agreed upon and refined. As a military planner for Operation Just Cause (U.S. 1989 intervention in Panama) pointed out, air command and control relationships for the operation required six months of planning. Even so, the integration of U.S. Air Force and Army efforts remains primarily at the corps level.

Marines sought their own tactical air because gaining air superiority over the landing area has been the primary consideration when establishing forces ashore. A landing on the shores of a hostile nation is likely to invoke an immediate and violent response from enemy air, and it is the initial phases of the operation that are most vulnerable to disruption by air. Shipping, for example, will be more concentrated than at any other time. The missile attack on the USS *Stark* (FFG-31) in 1987 serves as a recent reminder of the possible havoc even one aircraft might cause in such an operation. Marine tactical aircraft must therefore attempt to destroy hostile aircraft as far forward as possible. It is in the first phases of the operation that the air-ground task force will be heavily dependent on tactical aircraft to suppress and destroy enemy ground defenses. This will be even more true in the future, given the continued reduction in naval gunfire support. Nevertheless, tactical aircraft must remain ready to respond to hostile air attacks; Marine multirole F/A-18s provide the flexibility to meet these demands.

Air defense coverage should be extended as far out as possible with its limits usually coinciding with the force beach head line—the Marine Air Ground Task Force commander's tactical limit of responsibility. This encompasses a much broader area than ground forces could secure and, with missile systems, is designed to protect the vulnerable logistics buildup on the beach and other MAGTF elements.

Marine tactical aviation is the force multiplier that enables Marine Air Ground Task Forces to assume expanded missions. As a comparison, a Marine Expeditionary Force possesses five times more ordnance throw-weight than does an airborne division.[5]

Given this considerable power concentrated in one force, the task force can provide the economy-of-force so critical in the earliest stages of major regional conflicts—in essence, holding until the arrival of requisite follow-on forces. Less than one month after the invasion of Kuwait, I MEF assumed the northernmost defensive positions along the likely avenue of approach for the Iraqi Army—the high-speed coastal routes in Saudi Arabia. Had it been necessary, I MEF would have used extensive close air support in conjunction with ground forces to counter a numerically superior Iraqi attack. In the initial days of Desert Shield, the ability of Marine tactical aircraft to deliver close air support was not only critical to I MEF's ground defenses, but to the defense of Saudi

Arabia as well. Destroying the enemy as far forward as possible is always preferred, but close air support provides an insurance policy in the event time does not allow interdiction targeting.

A Marine Air Ground Task Force can deploy rapidly because so much of its fire power is provided by tactical aviation. The concept is described by the following passage from *The Air Campaign* by Colonel John A. Warden, U.S. Air Force: ". . . close air support was a substitute for something which could be done with more divisions or more artillery if they were available."[6] The statement implies the long-held Air Force contention that close air support should not be a substitute for heavy artillery.

In the case of the Marine Corps, however, it is not feasible to deploy "more divisions and artillery" rapidly. Instead, the Marine Corps relies on tactical aviation's considerable fire power to compensate for a light and more readily deployable ground force. As an example, 73% of I MEF's ordnance was delivered by Marine F/A-18s and A-6s during the Persian Gulf War.[7] Tactical aircraft moved relatively easily to previously secured bases in a region, and two dedicated ships were available to transport intermediate maintenance activities, as well as the equipment to construct expeditionary air fields. Marine tactical aircraft also may operate from aircraft carriers.

Are Carriers Enough?

Land-based Marine tactical aircraft and carrier-based aviation are complementary; in effect, Marine tactical aviation further extends the naval air arm ashore. Only Marine Air Ground Task Forces can rapidly establish expeditionary basing ashore for Marine tactical aircraft *and* carrier-based aircraft, including interoperable logistics support and command and control systems. Navy and Marine aviators receive the same training, and subscribe to the same doctrine. Carrier aircraft can be refueled and rearmed at bases ashore, and Marine aircraft can be supported on board the carriers. Marines have long recognized the need for land-based tactical aircraft to compensate for the inherent limitations of carrier aviation. A 1940 Marine Corps doctrinal publication said: "It can readily be seen that dependence upon carrier-based aviation alone is generally unsound practice, and that whenever possible supporting shore bases should be established and used by the major part of the attacking air force."[8]

In the case of Marine Expeditionary Units (Special Operations Capable), which have their own AV-8Bs only periodically, carrier aviation can provide sufficient support because of the limited nature of operations. The carrier's ability to generate air support for larger-scale operations ashore, however, is limited by the complex choreography of cyclic operations. Unlike the comparatively simple shore-based procedures, the process of launching aircraft from carriers requires the ships to devote considerable time and effort to managing the positioning, launching, rendezvous, recovery, and rearming of its aircraft. As a result, carriers normally generate fewer sorties per unit of time compared to land bases operating an equal number of aircraft.

According to the recent Department of the Navy *Integrated Amphibious Operations and Marine Air Support Requirements Study,* for example, a Marine Expeditionary Force in sustained operations in a high-threat environment would require 366 carrier-based F/A-18s (the equivalent of almost eight carrier air wings' worth of F/A-18s) to generate the same number of sorties as 75 shore-based aircraft.

The problem of providing enough responsive air support may be further compounded by threats that cause the carriers to stand farther off shore, requiring longer transit times for aircraft. In the worst case, the carriers might conceivably have to withdraw from the objective area. Those who contend that Marines should rely solely on carrier-based aircraft for fixed-wing support often argue that "Guadalcanal was a long time ago . . . ," referring to the situation in 1942 during which the Japanese threat caused the Navy to withdraw carrier support for Marines ashore for a time. Carriers today, though, face more threats along the littorals of the world than in those days—primarily because of the proliferation of modern weapon technology.

Forty-six nations possess the kinds of naval mines that repeatedly posed a problem to Coalition forces in the Persian Gulf War. Diesel submarines, now operated by many Third World countries, including Iran, significantly challenge antisubmarine warfare efforts, and ultimately the carriers. During the Falklands War, the Royal Navy carrier *Hermes* was attacked by an Argentine diesel submarine, albeit unsuccessfully, while operating in a confined area. Land-based air also poses a formidable threat to the carrier for reasons already stated. From August 1990 to January 1991, U.S. aircraft carriers remained outside the Persian Gulf and a considerable distance from I MEF—which was deployed along the Saudi-Kuwaiti border—because of concern for such threats. Under similar conditions, the carriers' ability to provide air support for the Marine Air Ground Task Force will be further diminished by the requirement to dedicate sorties to the carriers' defense. Guadalcanal may have been a long time ago, but its lessons are still relevant.

Given of carrier limitations, land-based tactical aviation has repeatedly proven itself essential to sea control and power projection along littorals. The land-based "Cactus Air Force" at Guadalcanal proved crucial in gaining air superiority. In recent planning for a campaign on NATO's northern flank, Vice Admiral Henry C. Mustin, then Commander Striking Fleet, Atlantic, referred to the Norwegian Sea and coast as having a "Siamese twin" relationship: both had to be defended to gain sea control. The Norway air-landed Marine Expeditionary Brigade with a Marine aircraft group carrier-equivalent on the coastal flank, augmented the fleet, as well as providing its landward defense. During the absence of carriers from the Persian Gulf in Desert Shield, Marine tactical aircraft from I MEF flew combat air patrols over the area, contributing significantly to sea control.

The need for land-based naval aviation will increase as the defense budget requires more cost-effective alternatives for power projection and sea control near the littorals. The carrier has been the Navy's mainstay in maintaining forward presence and responding to crises, and this role will continue. The problem in the future, however, will be in generating reinforcements for forward-deployed carriers responding to major regional conflicts. In 1948 when it was more readily apparent that carriers alone were insufficient to support major operations ashore, the U.S. Navy had 26 carriers. Tomorrow's base force will have only 12 carriers, and the likelihood of further reductions looms. Land-based Marine tactical aviation, with its ready deployability and interoperability, provides a cost-effective means of augmenting carrier-based air, particularly if the number of carriers declines.

Enabling Air Power

The expeditionary capabilities of the Marine Air Ground Task Force and its tactical aircraft will be increasingly important to the enablement of U.S. air power in major conflict. The Air Force's document *Global Reach—Global Power,* describes that service's impressive ability to conduct long-range air strikes against targets anywhere on the globe, a capability unquestionably demonstrated when B-52 bombers launched strikes against Iraq from Barksdale Air Force Base, Louisiana. Reducing the distance to the target, however, improves the effectiveness of a theater counter-air effort. From a tactical standpoint, advanced bases must be established to permit concentrating forces forward and achieving greater responsiveness. Defense analyst Jeffrey Record identified air power as ". . . the fulcrum of the military victory over Iraq." But, as he and others have noted, "Neither Desert Shield nor Desert Storm would have been possible without extensive USAF access to Saudi and other Gulf state bases."[9] The Air Force is very much an instrument of war and requires the extensive support associated with its purpose. The Air Force benefited from prepositioning of $1 billion-worth of equipment and stocks at its 12 air bases in the theater. As Record and former chief of staff General Michael Dugan, U.S. Air Force (Retired), also noted, "It is unlikely that the unique set of conditions that made the Desert Storm air war possible will ever be repeated again."[10]

Future host-nation support will be highly conditional in a world where allies feel less compelled to support U.S. military ventures than during the Cold War. For example, France, even in that era, denied U.S. aircraft access to its air space in the Libyan air strike of 1986. The environment may more closely approximate that of the 1920s–30s, when the U.S. lacked overseas basing and required the capability to seize and hold bases.[11]

A highly mobile, expeditionary force with its own air arm will likely prove to be a valuable asset for unified commanders facing more threats with fewer forward deployed forces. Such a force provides the theater commanders in chief with the most complete and readily employable combined arms force at the tactical level. As land-based naval aviation, it is a vital complement to carrier aviation in power projection and sea control near the littorals. In major regional conflicts, Marine tactical aviation enables the establishment of the Air Force in an austere theater. Few supporting arms are as versatile as Marine TacAir, and it is this versatility that provides the greatest savings.

Notes

1. Senate floor speech by Senator Sam Nunn entitled "The Defense Department Must Thoroughly Overhaul The Services Roles And Missions," 2 July 1992.

2. House of Representatives, 82nd Congress, 1st Session, "Fixing the Personnel Strength of the United States Marine Corps, Adding the Commandant as a Member of the Joint Chiefs of Staff," Report No. 666, 30 June 1951, p. 7.

3. Maj. John E. Valliere, USAF, "Stop Quibbling: Win the War," *Proceedings,* December 1990, p. 39.

4. Benjamin Franklin Cooling, Ed., *Case Studies in the Development of Close Air Support* (Office of Air Force History: Washington, D.C., 1990). See particularly Allan R. Millet, pp. 345–410, and I. B. Holley, pp. 535–555.

5. Advanced Amphibious Study Group, *Planners Reference Manual* Volume I, Quantico, Virginia, 1983 p. 2-5-2.

6. Col. John A. Warden III, *The Air Campaign* (National Defense University: Washington, D.C., 1988), pp. 104–105.
7. Headquarters, U.S. Marine Corps internal staffing document.
8. FMFRP 12-31, *Marine Corps Aviation: Amphibious Warfare,* republished by the Marine Corps Combat Development Center, Quantico, Virginia, 11 June 1990. For more recent treatments, see RAdm. Martin D. Carmody, USN (Ret.), "The CVs Are Not Enough," *Proceedings,* January 1990, pp. 106–107. Also, Benjamin F. Schemmer, "Six Carriers Launch only 17% of Attack Missions in Desert Storm," *Armed Forces Journal,* January 1992, p. 12; and RAdm. R.D. Mixson, USN, "Navy's Version of Carrier Contribution to Desert Storm," *Armed Forces Journal,* February 1992, p. 44.
9. Jeffrey Record, "Why The Air War Worked," *Armed Forces Journal,* April 1991 p. 45.
10. Gen. Michael J. Dugan, USAF (Ret), "First Lessons of Victory," *U.S. News and World Report,* 18 March 1991, pp. 5–7.
11. Report of the Future Security Environment Working Group, Commission on Integrated Long Term Strategy, Washington, D.C., 1988.

Colonel Linn, a graduate of the Virginia Military Institute with a Masters from Georgetown, currently is serving in Headquarters, Marine Corps.

INDEX

A-4 Skyhawks: Dewey Canyon operation and, 114; Jet-Assisted Take-off for, 69; Khe Sanh campaign and, 111; reconnaissance teams and, 116; with reduced fuel loads, 102; replacements, 79; TPQ radar and, 92; in Vietnam, 70, 71, 119
A-6A aircraft, 79, 92, 97, 99, 114, 119
AH-1/AH-1G helicopters, 80, 106–7, 116, 119
The Air Campaign (Warden), 151
Air Force, U.S.: on close air support, 52–53; Da Nang Air Base and, 66; on JFACC, 138, 141–43; Khe Sanh campaign and, 111; landing operations and, 48; Marine Corps doctrine and, 137; Marine tactical aviation and, 148–49; single management in Vietnam and, 85–88; Skyspot radar of, 92; tactical air support study and, 81, 82; TDCC on Monkey Mountain and, 90–91; understanding Marines by, 140; Vietnam surface-to-air missile sites and, 99–100

Air Support Radar Teams (ASRTs), 92, 93
aircraft carriers, 7, 48, 133, 151–54
air-ground operations: first (1919), 1; integration of, 149; in Nicaragua, 29–32, 36–41; 3d Brigade in China and, 15. *See also* close air support
Amphibious Assault Bulk Fuel Handling System (AABFHS), 68
amphibious operations, 6, 15, 25, 37–38, 48, 152. *See also* Third Marine Amphibious Force
Amphibious Ready Group, Seventh Fleet, 62
An Hoa airfield, Vietnam, 76, 93
Anderson, Norman J., 111, 112
Anderson, Richard, 76
Armstrong, Alan J., 119
Army, U.S.: Air Force integration with, 149; on air power, 3; in China (1920s), 4, 8; in Korea, 55–56; tactical air support study and, 81, 82; TDCC on Monkey Mountain and, 90–91
Army Air Corps, 18, 48

29–32, 36–41; lessons learned in, 24–25; Marine air operations, 13; Marine aviators in, 19, 20, 47; Marines ambushed while tracking Sandino, 34–36; Sandino strikes back at Marines, 33–34; U.S. participation in civil war in, 27, 28
Nicaraguan Air Force, 31
Nickerson, Herman, Jr., 118
9th Marine Expeditionary Brigade (9thMEB), 63, 65
Nixon, Richard, 117
Noble, John D., 70
Norway, north Approaches to, 131–33, 153
Norwegian Air Force, 125–26
Nueva Segovia, Nicaragua, 34, 39
Nunn, Sam, 147

O-1 aircraft, 58, 96, 114, 119
O-2 aircraft, 96
Obenhaus, Leon E., 62
Observation Squadrons, 7, 14, 25
Ocotal, Nicaragua, 29–32, 40
offensive air support, tactical air support and, 82
OL-6 amphibians, 6, 15, 25
OL-8 amphibians, 37–38
Olongapo Naval Base, Philippines, 6, 7, 8
Omnibus Agreement for Command and Control of USMC Tactical Airpower, 137, 139–40, 142–43
Operation Double Eagle, 109–10
Operation Hastings, 110
Operation Just Cause, 149
operational direction: single management in Vietnam (1968–1970) and, 86, 88
Operations Air Support Center (OASC), 91
operations ashore: establishing, Marine tactical aviation and, 149–50; sustained, carrier-based vs. land-based air support for, 152–53; sustained, JFACC and, 139–40

ordnance, shortages of, 98
Oriskany, 98
O'Shea, George, 33–34
OV-10A aircraft, 96, 101, 106, 114, 116, 119

Pacifier operations, 116
Page, Arthur H., Jr., 10–11
Panama, U.S. intervention (1989), 149
Peking, China, 8, 11, 16, 17–18
Persian Gulf War, 150, 151, 153, 154–55
Phu Bai airfield, 71–72, 73, 75, 77, 87, 91, 93
Pierce, F. E., 37
Platt, Jonas M., 109
Prairie series of operations, Vietnam, 110
Princeton, 58, 63

Quang Ngai, Vietnam, 59, 73, 76
Quang Tri helicopter base, Vietnam, 75, 93, 114
Quantico, Marine Corps Development Center at, 67
Quilter, Charles J., 112, 115

radar: MPQ-14, 92; RABFAC, 97, 120; Skyspot, 92; TPQ-10, 92, 113, 114, 120
Rathbun, Robert L., 58
Raymond, Morrison, Knudson-Brown, Root, and Jones (RMK-BRJ), 72
RAZOR, 113
reconnaissance: aircraft, 80, 101, 114, 119; insertion and extraction for, 115–16; Smedley and, 15–17, 18; tactical air support and, 82–83; in Vietnam, 99–101; by VMCJ-1, 64, 74, 99, 118
Record, Jeffrey, 154–55
Reusser, Kenneth L., 54
RF-4/RF-4B aircraft, 80, 114, 119
RF-8/RF-8A/RF-8B aircraft, 101, 119
Richal, M. A., 34, 35

SERIES EDITOR

THOMAS J. CUTLER has been serving the U.S. Navy in various capacities for more than fifty years. The author of many articles and books, including several editions of *The Bluejacket's Manual* and *A Sailor's History of the U.S. Navy,* he is currently the director of professional publishing at the Naval Institute Press and Fleet Professor of Strategy and Policy with the Naval War College. He has received the William P. Clements Award for Excellence in Education as military teacher of the year at the U.S. Naval Academy, the Alfred Thayer Mahan Award for Naval Literature, the U.S. Maritime Literature Award, the Naval Institute Press Author of the Year Award, and the Commodore Dudley Knox Lifetime Achievement Award in Naval History.

The **Naval Institute Press** is the book-publishing arm of the U.S. Naval Institute, a private, nonprofit, membership society for sea service professionals and others who share an interest in naval and maritime affairs. Established in 1873 at the U.S. Naval Academy in Annapolis, Maryland, where its offices remain today, the Naval Institute has members worldwide.

Members of the Naval Institute support the education programs of the society and receive the influential monthly magazine *Proceedings* or the colorful bimonthly magazine *Naval History* and discounts on fine nautical prints and on ship and aircraft photos. They also have access to the transcripts of the Institute's Oral History Program and get discounted admission to any of the Institute-sponsored seminars offered around the country.

The Naval Institute's book-publishing program, begun in 1898 with basic guides to naval practices, has broadened its scope to include books of more general interest. Now the Naval Institute Press publishes about seventy titles each year, ranging from how-to books on boating and navigation to battle histories, biographies, ship and aircraft guides, and novels. Institute members receive significant discounts on the Press' more than eight hundred books in print.

Full-time students are eligible for special half-price membership rates. Life memberships are also available.

For a free catalog describing Naval Institute Press books currently available, and for further information about joining the U.S. Naval Institute, please write to:

Member Services
U.S. NAVAL INSTITUTE
291 Wood Road
Annapolis, MD 21402-5034
Telephone: (800) 233-8764
Fax: (410) 571-1703
Web address: www.usni.org